PIMPS, WHORES
AND
WELFARE BRATS

PIMPS, WHORES
AND
WELFARE BRATS

THE STUNNING
CONSERVATIVE TRANSFORMATION
OF A FORMER WELFARE QUEEN

STAR PARKER
WITH LORENZO BENET

INTRODUCTION BY RUSH LIMBAUGH

POCKET BOOKS
New York   London   Toronto   Sydney   Tokyo   Singapore

POCKET BOOKS, a division of Simon & Schuster Inc.
1230 Avenue of the Americas, New York, NY 10020

Copyright © 1997 by Star Parker
Introduction copyright © 1997 by Rush Limbaugh

ISBN: 0-671-53465-3

First Pocket Books hardcover printing February 1997

10 9 8 7 6 5 4 3 2 1

POCKET and colophon are registered trademarks of
Simon & Schuster Inc.

Printed in the U.S.A.

To my wonderful husband, Peter,
and my beautiful daughters, Angel and Rachel.
Your love helped me achieve my dream.

ACKNOWLEDGMENTS

This book would not have been possible to complete without the support and encouragement of many terrific people. Their faith kept me focused and motivated during one and a half years of research and writing. They did it all, everything from lending moral support to engaging me in a constructive debate to inspire my thoughts and words.

My collaborator, Lorenzo Benet, distilled my life story and then helped strengthen my arguments by challenging the political positions that appear in the last third of the book.

Literary agent Scott Waxman envisioned the book after seeing a newspaper article about me. His colleague at The Literary Group, Frank Weimann, then found the perfect individual to oversee this project from start to finish, Pocket Books Senior Editor Sue Carswell, whose energy and effective insights touched every page of this manuscript. Others at Pocket provided their invaluable assistance: Editorial Director Emily Bestler; Managing Editors Donna O'Neill and Donna Ruvituso; my publicists, Liz Hartman and Cindy Ratzlaff; and Craig Hillman. Thank you all.

If I could give one thing to every American, it would be Rush Limbaugh's faith in the free market system and "rugged individualism" as the keys to overcoming any obstacle. Thanks, Rush, and you too, Kit.

ACKNOWLEDGMENTS

Pastor Fred Price, your Sunday sermons challenged me both personally and professionally. Pat Buchanan, my journey would have hit a few more bumps in the road if you hadn't invited me four years ago to your American Cause conference on New Conservatism. Rosey Grier, you have been such a dear friend and done so much for Peter and me that I'd gladly block for you if you ever wanted to take a turn running the football. Last but not least, many thanks to Alan Keyes, a great friend and an inspiration to all. You are a wonderful moral leader for our times.

CONTENTS

CONTENTS

Seeth thou a man diligent in his business?
He shall stand before kings; he shall
not stand before obscure men.

Proverbs 22:29

INTRODUCTION

I remember my first introduction to Star Parker. It was early 1994 and she was on television with a group of about twenty black Republicans who were extolling the virtues of conservative ideas that could go a long way toward ending poverty in the United States. The consensus among the speakers was that the Democratic Party and the traditional black civil rights leadership had failed miserably in their attempt to end urban decay. Democrats were supposed to have had all the answers, but in the inner cities, unemployment was high, schools were not educating our children, and crime was rampant. A reporter in the audience asked, "How did it get like this?" It was quiet for a moment and then Star Parker stepped up to the microphone, smartly dressed as always in a gray skirt and matching blazer, and went on to provide a brilliant answer. In essence, she said, blacks were so happy that black elected officials were in power, people weren't paying attention to what the politicians were doing.

Star went on to talk about entrepreneurship and the desperate need for legislation that would cut government red tape and deregulate small businesses. This would foster an environment for self-starters. In my opinion, she's right on because only in this arena can rugged individualism and self-reliance bear fruit and derail the socialistic redistribution of wealth that has crippled the self-initiative required to achieve the American Dream.

I believe the American Dream is alive for any American willing to work hard and break through barriers blocking the path to prosperity. Which brings me to Star Parker, and why every American should read her inspirational story, controversial as it may be in the black community.

Star is a product of Aid to Families with Dependent Children, and contrary to what one might presume about a former welfare recipient, she is dead set against any welfare reform proposal that maintains the status quo and extends benefits indefinitely to all comers. Star feels welfare is an insidious parasite that sucks self-reliance dry at its best, and at its worst is responsible for the deterioration of urban America. As government remains paralyzed in an acrimonious debate over how to shape welfare reform, we need only look at Star's life, and that of others like her, to find the solution.

Let me tell you a little bit about Star. The third of five children, she is the daughter of a retired beautician and a noncommissioned officer of the United States Air Force. Growing up, she followed her itinerant father from her birthplace of Moses Lake, Washington, to rural Indiana, to Japan, to riot-torn East St. Louis, Illinois, and then to Mount Holly, New Jersey. There, her family settled in a low-income African-American neighborhood not far from McGuire Air Force Base.

As a teenager, Star was a delinquent. She joined a gang, cut school, disobeyed her parents, used drugs, torched a teacher's car, was arrested for shoplifting, and got into all kinds of other scrapes too numerous to mention here. She lived a hard life and had her share of run-ins with racist authority figures. Barely literate, she graduated from public high school in 1975. Believing a college degree was beyond her grasp, Star moved to Los Angeles and quickly immersed herself in the life of a party girl. She got pregnant and had an abortion. However, she was a fast learner. Within her reach was a government welfare system that rewarded indigent, unmarried pregnant women with a monthly government check until they got around to getting their government-paid abortion. When Star got pregnant again, she decided to go for it.

In all, Star underwent four abortions, collecting AFDC welfare most of the way. After getting pregnant a fifth time in 1980 at the age of twenty-three, she decided to keep her child and raise her on her own. Instead of moving back home to live with mom and dad, or giving up her baby for adoption, she knew where to turn: Uncle Sam. In the short term, Star discovered that by collecting $465 a month in assistance, plus food stamps, and by getting a part-time job that paid her under the table, she could earn far more money with less effort than working an honest forty-hour week. She even made extra income by selling her Medi-Cal stickers on the black market. Star stayed on AFDC welfare for three and a half straight years.

When it comes to maximizing individual achievement, people draw on different sources of inspiration to overcome any obstacles. Some are motivated into action by a book or an encounter with a mentor. Others are thrust into adversity and capitalize on an inner well of strength where none was believed to have ever existed. And still others, like Star Parker, find their inspiration in their faith in the Divine Creator. Star joined a Christian church and began leading a lifestyle premised on the teachings of the Bible. This experience gave her the courage to quit welfare cold turkey. Star didn't know how she was going to pay the rent or find the money to buy groceries for herself and her three-year-old daughter. Fortunately, she had recently earned her college degree and was able to find work as a customer service representative. An education can do that for you. The pay wasn't much, but it was more than she collected from welfare. On the job, Star learned she wasn't cut out for a career answering phones. She wanted to be her own boss and she came up with an idea.

There are places in this world where government largesse and repression crush ideas, where a lengthy prison sentence is the reward for displaying self-initiative. Star came to realize that in America, a country that promotes economic and political freedom, she could put her ideas to work. As a young Christian, she noticed that it was difficult to meet other churchgoers like herself. There were plenty of social activities, but no place for people to turn to find out what was going on in a given weekend. Star took the initiative to create a magazine that published a calendar of events for young single Christians like herself. She had no income to start up her business, but she had friends willing to lend her a hand and a supportive group of ministers who wanted to see her succeed. What's more, Star Parker had the newly inspired Star Parker. She borrowed a typewriter from a neighbor to write copy and solicited her own ads from churches and businesses. A friend from church who printed the magazines agreed to let Star pay on an installment basis until she had the cash flow to pay her bills on time. She had her share of missteps, but within a year, she was depositing more advertising revenue in a month than she used to see in a year from AFDC welfare.

Her magazine, entitled *Not Forsaking the Assembling*, would grow to sixty-four pages and go on to become an influential player in the social and political circles of South Los Angeles. If her story ended here, it would be remarkable enough, but it doesn't. In April 1992, the Los Angeles riots broke out and thieves and thugs plundered and burned Star's advertisers and distributors. In the aftermath, as Star laid off her employees and contemplated folding up shop, she got a dose of Democratic political opportunism. She noticed that black leaders would not condemn the rioters. Instead, they held up these criminals as victims and blamed Republican policies for the chaos and destruction. She noticed that one politically correct, Corporation-for-Public-Broadcasting-funded radio show continually referred to the riots as "civil disturbances." Liberals everywhere used the term "civil disobedience" to describe what had happened. Black leaders, Congressional Democrats, and the liberal media justified the burning, looting, and more than fifty deaths, explaining it all away as the expected reaction to decades of racial oppression.

Star Parker wasn't buying any of it. She went on the offensive and challenged the traditional black leadership and the then Democratic-controlled Congress. They had seized on the tragedy to demonize twelve years of Republican leadership and lobby for programs that rewarded the rioters who caused the mess in the first place. The liberals failed to acknowledge that thirty years of blundered Great Society programs and a few trillion dollars pumped into the inner cities had not only failed to cure the ills, but made them worse. Star Parker recognized this and had the courage to speak out at a time when many blacks who agreed with her in spirit remained silent.

Star could not resurrect her magazine, but her conservative views resonated with television and radio audiences. Requests poured in from the media and organizations that wanted to hear her message. To combat urban blight, Star created an organization called the Coalition on Urban Affairs to promote conservative solutions, such as limited government, private school vouchers, and strong moral standards.

Along the way, Star's talking has gotten her in trouble with some black leaders. It also got her some respect. Star, a wonderful public speaker, has hosted daily issue-theme radio talk shows in San Francisco and Los Angeles, addressed the delegates at the 1996 Republican National Convention in San Diego, and was profiled in a documentary produced by the British Broadcasting Corporation.

One thing Star was too shy to talk about at the 1994 press conference on black conservatism was that she is proof that America works. Not even the specter of institutional racism looms large enough to hold back any honest, hardworking person who aspires to achieve the dream. Turn the page and you'll find out how Star did it, and you'll be wonderfully entertained in the process. You'll also find out what's holding everyone else back.

Rush Limbaugh

PART 1

A STAR IS BORN

1

I CAN'T CRY RACISM

Almost four years ago, I was sitting at home on my patio in south Orange County, California, pondering my next career move. I had moved there from Los Angeles with my husband and two children shortly after the 1992 Los Angeles riots. Actually, it was more like an escape. We needed a break from the racial tension that had plagued our old neighborhood in Koreatown, and we also needed to regroup after the folding of a monthly social policy and religion magazine I had published for eight years.

It was your typical Southern California fall day. A cool breeze was coming off the Pacific Ocean and the blue, sun-splashed skies went on for miles and miles. I was about to step out for a walk with my family when the phone rang. The woman on the other end introduced herself as Bay Buchanan, sister of 1992 Republican presidential candidate Pat Buchanan, and subsequently a 1996 presidential candidate. At the time, I was a political innocent as far as Washington politics were concerned, so his name was only vaguely familiar. As Bay checked off the highlights of her brother's résumé—

political aide to both President Richard Nixon and President Ronald Reagan, cohost of a Cable News Network debate show, and syndicated columnist—I was becoming quite impressed. What she didn't know was that I had never even watched CNN or ever listened to talk radio. Admittedly, I was a little embarrassed to tell her she was recruiting a novice. Then I remembered where I had heard this man Pat Buchanan's name before. I had read about him in the newspaper and it had portrayed him as a racist and an extremist. Still, I wanted to hear Bay out.

She certainly had done her homework on me. Bay had seen a story written about me that had run in *The Washington Times.* In it, I explained how I got off Aid to Families with Dependent Children and started my own magazine for young black Christians. I also was quoted as calling for the "abolition of welfare."

Bay asked if I would come and speak at her brother's conference on New Conservatism in Washington, D.C. Though in my magazine I had written editorials protesting abortion and the distribution of condoms to school children, I was a political outsider with no formal party affiliation. I knew my personal politics coincided with Republican values, but I wasn't anxious to court the GOP's inner circle. I had to wonder whether the good old boys' club would really want to listen to a brash and outspoken black woman, especially a conservative one like myself. As for a past? Whoa—boy, did I have a *big* one. So when Bay Buchanan extended the invitation, my first reaction was "Girlfriend, aren't you making a mistake?"

I politely declined and hung up. But Bay, the former U.S. Treasurer under President Ronald Reagan, was not put off that easily. She kept calling back and insisted I was the right person to speak out for women in the conservative movement. She said, "Star, as my brother said at the last Republican National Convention, we are in a cultural war . . . and we need you because there are black people in this country who can't cry racism, black people who have experienced the American Dream and know that this country can work for all people."

In the end, I decided to go because I was curious about the type of response I might get. As an added bonus, I got an all-expense-paid trip to the nation's capital for myself and my family. When I travel, I love taking along my two girls, and I was especially excited about going to D.C. because I would be able to show them the Lincoln Memorial. Also, it wasn't every day that we got to stay in a grandiose hotel like the Washington Hilton, the site of Pat Buchanan's conference.

On Friday, November 11, 1993, I arrived in Washington, D.C., with my husband, Peter Parker, and our daughters, Rachel, then eight, and Angel, then thirteen. Angel is the product of an old and brief relationship with a boyfriend I had met in journalism class while attending Los Angeles City College in 1980. Her father is black. She's thin like me and has her father's light coloring. Peter is white and our daughter Rachel is a beautiful mulatto girl with dark curly hair and a lovely smile.

After landing at National Airport and driving past Capitol Hill, we checked into the Hilton, a gorgeous concrete and glass hotel overlooking the Washington Monument. The lobby was breathtaking, a magnificent horizontal atrium with a giant crystal chandelier suspended from a domed entryway.

That night, the Buchanans were hosting a gathering at their stately southern colonial home in McLean, Virginia, with some of the movers and shakers of the Beltway. As we approached Pat's house, it reminded me of the plantation mansions I had seen as a little girl while visiting my grandmother in South Carolina. I thought, "Aha, he's gotta be a racist!" But when my husband and I were introduced to Pat and his wife, I didn't experience a negative vibe at all: in fact, Pat was very gracious and polite. His wife, Shelley, was courteous and reminded me of a porcelain Southern belle doll. I left that night with a positive impression of Pat, though I wondered if he would feel the same way about me the next day. Because child—did I have a speech planned for that conservative man!

The next morning, we all gathered in the hotel conference room. I sat through a speech on the culture of dependency by *Losing Ground* author Charles Murray, who would later publish *The Bell Curve*. Then I heard conservative economist Lewellyn Rockwell, who had written the 1990 book *The Economics of Liberty*. When it was my turn to take the podium, Pat stood up and introduced me to the crowd:

"In 1984, after three and a half years on AFDC welfare, Star Parker took a turn in life and founded *N.F.T.A.*, a Christian magazine, and turned it into a thriving publication while giving voice to traditional pro-family conservative views in the black community. After the LA riots, she founded the Coalition on Urban Affairs to make sure that the conservative response to the riots was heard."

I got up from my seat and took my spot behind the microphone. As I clutched my notes and looked out into the enormous ballroom, I felt nervous. I did not see one black face in the audience. All eyes were upon me, this dark-brown slender woman with a star cut out in the silver cap on her right front tooth. For a moment, I felt like Whoopi Goldberg at a convention for the Ancient Order of Hibernians. In my bright red dress and matching giant hoop earrings, I looked more like I was ready to go dancing on *Soul Train* than give a speech to several hundred white, mostly male Republicans.

Then I took a deep breath and began: "We have two economic systems working for America: capitalism for the rich and socialism for the poor. The problem with a government that lets both systems operate is that the middle class gets stuck working for the rich to support the poor."

I went on to share my story: how after getting pregnant in

1978, I became the first member of my family, and all of our ancestors, to sign up for AFDC welfare. For me, that bi-monthly check became a cushion that enabled me to avoid responsibility. Had it not arrived in my mailbox on the first and fifteenth of every month, I wonder if I would have gotten pregnant four times and had four abortions. I wonder if I would have sought help from my family instead of dismissing them as out of step with my hip lifestyle. You see, I got caught up in the welfare cycle, seduced by the easy living and the carefree allure that allowed me to do as I pleased. It would take me almost six years to break free from its magical, sometimes luxurious hold.

I didn't have the courage to quit until I became a Christian. At first, I got a part-time clerical job, but later I launched a magazine to serve as a social calendar for single churchgoers like myself. Over time, it evolved into a local mass-market publication covering religion, social policy, and entrepreneurism in the Los Angeles black community.

My first exposure to politics came in 1991 when I worked with the Traditional Values Coalition. I was helping organize demonstrations and lobbying the Los Angeles School Board to keep condoms out of public schools. It was a personal crusade: my oldest daughter was attending junior high at the time and I did not support a learning environment that advocated handing out contraceptives to kids. From there, I joined a campaign to convince California voters to support a ballot initiative that would award families taxpayers' dollars to send their children to private schools using vouchers.

In the spring of 1992, shortly after the Los Angeles riots, my magazine almost folded because most of my key advertisers and distribution outlets were burned to the ground. I had to lay off seven employees. Yet when I turned on the television, did I see local and national black leaders condemning the lawlessness and violence? No, they were too busy blaming past Republican administrations for the catastrophe, and hustling

Washington politicians to create more government jobs to keep young gangsters off the streets. I'm all for job development, but I resent programs that promote government dependency. Urban America was already too reliant on taxpayers. What was needed was participation from the private sector and policies that would nourish neighborhood stability, such as lower taxes, moral guidelines for our children, school choice, welfare reform, and less regulation of private inner-city businesses. Some people call these principles "conservative." Forget that—I call them common sense.

I told Pat's crowd that they were not alone; urban America was full of people just like them, including millions of blacks who support conservative values, but who feel compelled to vote Democratic because that was the Party that saved our butts during the civil rights movement in the 1960s.

So on that November day at the Washington Hilton as I was winding down my speech at the conference on New Conservatism, I turned to Pat and said, "You can eat your lox while I'm enjoying my ham hocks, but we gotta work together to win this cultural war." I looked around the room at all the suits and preppie haircuts. "You talk about new conservatives, and to you, I probably sound like one of the old ones. Well, not exactly. You all went through Georgetown and I went through the 'hood!"

I realized, however, it didn't matter where we were born or where we went to school. I explained to the audience that the challenge ahead was finding common ground and breaking down barriers, like color and ethnicity. Only by encouraging diversity can the conservative movement grow. And by inviting more blacks to sit at the round table, we'll add a new dimension not only to the GOP, but to the future of America.

The crowd stopped me fourteen times to applaud. At the very end, I got a standing ovation. Tears welled up in my eyes and I quickly went to my seat because I was afraid I was about to start bawling. When I had accepted Bay's invitation to speak, I truly didn't know what to expect and this was more than I had ever anticipated.

I felt reinvigorated by the conference on New Conservatism. In the three years since that speech, I have traveled the country, speaking before people from all walks of life. I have visited Ivy League schools in the East and Christian Coalition conferences in the West. At every stop, I find I'm not the only one tired of sitting idly by as our nation continues to go under. On the national scene, I discovered that as a black woman espousing conservative values, I was viewed as an oxymoron. Yet much of middle America is screaming, "We've had enough! No more of this nonsense!" Those voices were finally heard on November 8, 1994, (and once again in this past election) when Americans put the Republican Party in charge of Congress for the first time in forty years.

After the election, there was this notion out there that Republicans swept Congress on the backs of angry white males. Yet I, as a black woman, had spent the previous year aggressively rallying support for conservatism and the Republican Party. Those naysayers were forgetting the record number of blacks who broke ranks and voted for the Grand Old Party.

Consider that in 1994 conservative Wisconsin governor Tommy Thompson won reelection with 45 percent of the black vote. Even my own Republican-disguised-as-conservative governor, Pete Wilson, got a relatively high 20 percent of the black vote in California when he won reelection that same year. The revolt wasn't just by angry white men, and I sure didn't want to be excluded from the count.

I have a message for the Congressional Black Caucus and the civil rights leadership of yesterday. I am tired of the chronic complaining that black achievement is being undermined by institutional racism. How can that be when black teenagers are rejecting education in droves because excelling in the classroom is viewed as "being white"? What has institutional racism got to do with being called a "sell-out" if you work hard and aspire to live in a better neighborhood with safe streets and good schools? Many blacks reject conformity because they've heard it over and over again from their leaders that the institutionalized racist boogie man will step on them if they try to mainstream. So what's left for them? Raising their children in the "gangsta's paradise," where thugs set the rules? Must we rely on affirmative action for eternity to get our own piece of the dream?

Blacks cannot cry racism every time something doesn't go their way. Some are in bad circumstances because they made bad choices. Still, many blacks are living the American Dream and want it for their children's children. What many more need to recognize is that the dream—a decent-paying job, a safe neighborhood to raise a family in, and a future for their children—can be achieved only with limited government, educational choices, economic opportunity, and strong moral standards. That's conservatism, folks. Plain and simple.

2
MY LIFE AS A WELFARE BRAT

In April 1995, I went on Oprah Winfrey's show to debate two single welfare mothers who were named Linda and Dellamarie. Linda was from Milwaukee, Wisconsin, and had been collecting $248 a month from welfare for a decade to support herself and her ten-year-old son. Dellamarie, who lived in Cambridge, Massachusetts, was getting $855 in monthly welfare and food stamp benefits to provide for herself and her three children. She had been on and off welfare for eighteen years. They both felt that since they were raising children—a woman's most important job—taxpayers must provide them with paychecks.

Linda argued that welfare should assist her in the same way child support provides for divorced women and Social Security provides for widowed women. And since Linda believed she was *entitled* to benefits, she said she felt no duty to go out and work for her welfare check.

Entitlement! Ugh—there was that word raising its ugly little head again, lingering over these women like the smog that hangs over Los Angeles. As I sat on Oprah's stage facing these women, I shook my head in frustration as they whined about government plans that would force them to go to work. I didn't pretend for a moment to be sympathetic. Finally, when I couldn't take it another second (and I *am* the hollerin' kind!), I interrupted them and explained that they were the products of thirty years of liberal propaganda and personified everything that's wrong with the current welfare system.

When I was growing up, the people from my neighborhood who were on welfare viewed it as the last resort, not as an entitlement. It was perceived as a form of temporary relief. Yet today, women like Linda and Dellamarie have redefined welfare as an *alternative lifestyle.* I looked both of these women in the eye and told them it was unfair for them to be at home raising their kids with taxpayers' dollars while the rest of us were putting our children in day care so we could work to support them. "I do believe," I said, "that within your lifetime you will have friends, cousins, sisters—somebody— who will help you with your children while you go to work and hone your gifts and talents."

Linda and Dellamarie were shooting me dirty looks but the audience was cheering me on so I kept up the attack. The crowd let out a gasp when I told them about the nice one-bedroom apartment I could afford on my monthly $465 welfare check and how I earned extra cash selling my Medi-Cal stickers on the black market to friends and acquaintances instead of using them for myself. I explained that not everyone was doing this, but welfare, by its very nature, discouraged finding a job and fostered a take-what-you-can-get attitude. To me it was no longer getting some government money to tide me over in hard times. I believed I was owed that bimonthly check, and by golly, I was gonna get what belonged to me!

I said to Oprah, "Our current welfare system is like a sick baby. Now babies don't like medicine because it tastes nasty, but adults know what is best for their kids—they've got to swallow that medicine. But let me tell you, the American welfare system is so ill, the sickness is out of control, and it's highly contagious, too. The welfare system's got to take a large dose of medicine, even though it tastes bad."

It's not just the welfare mothers taking advantage, I told the crowd. Fathers recklessly abandon their families knowing full well the government will pick up the tab after they split. "We have given those men the incentive to abandon any responsibility because they know that cushion is there," I said.

I looked up and there was Oprah staring me down like a prizefighter. While I was in her ring I had come out swinging, and now she was ready to answer my first assault. "But you can't just throw women and children out on the streets," she countered, her arms crossed, clutching the microphone.

"No, we cannot," I said. "But you know what? Every time I hear that argument, I think back to when we were 4 million slaves set free without any government welfare program. We did not see babies dying in the streets. There was always room for one more in somebody's house. You can't convince me that given the financial position we're in, people won't kick in."

I told Oprah about my recent trip to Washington, D.C., where I had lobbied some Congressional political aides on welfare reform. "I talked to some ladies up there on the Hill, black women who I know are making seventy-five thousand dollars a year," I told the audience. "I had to ask them straight out, 'Are you going to let a baby die in the street?' What has happened to our faith in God? Our faith in each other? What has happened to our faith in our churches? What's actually happening is that the government is competing with our helping institutions."

Oprah wasn't satisfied with that response. She looked at me and asked the same question again, this time pointing at Linda, the welfare mom from Milwaukee. "Why must we have to see her in the street?"

Then I felt a surge from the audience like a wave rolling over the sand, and I sensed they were now getting behind Oprah. There was sympathy building up for these women who insisted they had a right to live off taxpayers because they wanted to be mommies. So I turned to Linda and said indignantly, "We don't have to see anyone in the streets. Linda, where's your mama?"

I heard the crowd go "Yeah! Yeah!" Now the momentum was swinging back to me. I could tell Linda was flustered. She said, "My mother feels the same way you do." And I said, "Where are your cousins? Where's your auntie? Where are your brothers? They're comfortable with the system taking care of you?"

Admittedly, I was a little hard on her. Maybe it was because listening to Linda and Dellamarie, I recognized somebody else in these two women: the old Star of long ago.

3

FAST TIMES AS A WELFARE QUEEN

I was born on November 25, 1956, Thanksgiving Day, in Moses Lake, Washington. My father's name is James Irby; he was a noncommissioned officer in the Air Force and served most of his time working as a flight steward. I was named Larstella, after my aunts Laura and Stella, my mother's younger sisters. I later learned *Stella* meant "star" in Italian, and that's how I eventually got my nickname. My mother's name was Essie Doris, but she preferred to go by Doris. She worked as a beautician most of her life. When I arrived, she and my father had been married for four years and already had two children: my sister, Avis, and my brother, Michael. They had two more kids after me, my sister Vera and my youngest brother, Eric. My father and mother had five mouths to feed and while we were far from rich, we never went hungry and we never stooped to accept government handouts. That was a point of pride for my father. But that blue-collar upbringing was totally lost on me.

I originally got turned on to welfare back in 1977. I was twenty-one years old and living on the wild side, which included a buffet table of exotic drugs, casual sex, and all-night parties. A typical day was spent hanging out by the basketball courts at Venice Beach, where the supply of sunshine, good-looking guys, and angel dust was plentiful. I was working a minimum-wage job processing camera film at a Fotomat store and living with a roommate in a small apartment in the mid-Wilshire district of Los Angeles, near Koreatown. My home was a transient neighborhood of young professionals—white, black, and Asian—living in one- and two-bedroom apartments jammed into brightly painted stucco buildings that were three stories high and covered half a city block. There was underground parking, and swimming pools and Jacuzzis in the courtyards. I got to admit, it was good living!

I got pregnant for the first time in 1977, which wasn't hard to do in those pre-AIDS, "why-bother-using-birth-control" days. As soon as my "free" clinic doctor gave me the news, I was pretty sure I was going to get an abortion because that's exactly what all my friends were doing. One night, I went out to a club and started telling my girlfriends I was knocked up. As I sipped on my rum and Coke, they told me not to worry and said, "Oh darlin', don't you know welfare will take care of you?"

Though AFDC welfare was administered by the federal, state, and county governments, everyone called it "going on the county" because the local program was run by the Los Angeles County Department of Public Social Services. According to my friends, I could receive Medi-Cal stickers for prenatal care, eye exams, and dental checkups, or I could use one of the stickers for an abortion. Since there was no way I was going to let a child interfere with my night life, I simply bought a Medi-Cal sticker from a girlfriend for $200 and used that to get the abortion. I didn't sign up right away for welfare. Part of me was too embarrassed to go through the process, but my pride was wearing thin.

Black market Medi-Cal stickers were easy to get if you knew someone on welfare. A single sticker for an abortion in the first trimester cost $200 on the sly. If you walked into a clinic cold without insurance, they charged $400 for the procedure.

Here is how the system was supposed to work: Once you verified your pregnancy, Medi-Cal issued you a monthly personalized card, roughly three by five inches in size, containing eight labels for various medical benefits. You were supposed to present the card at the clinic where you were being treated, and a nurse would peel off a sticker when she checked you in. What I discovered was that some clinics didn't require you to produce your card—just an unpeeled sticker—making it simple to have a hearing test, a cavity filled, or an abortion, using somebody else's sticker.

Before making the appointment for my abortion, I called my mother and confided in her, half expecting her to talk me out of it. She didn't object and kept a respectful distance. I sensed she felt I was an adult and old enough to make my own decisions. When I told her, she said, "Oh?" She had nothing more to say about it and I think part of me wanted her to throw a fit and show some rage. After that conversation, I never gave it another thought.

I called an abortion clinic located about half an hour away by bus from my apartment. There were clinics closer to my home, but I was instructed that you could use a black market sticker at this particular medical facility.

The clinic was housed in a small, one-story, brick medical annex next to a now defunct community hospital in the Crenshaw district of Los Angeles. I walked in and handed my girlfriend's sticker to a middle-aged black woman sitting behind a counter. I could tell by the look on her face that she knew it wasn't mine. I tensed up, expecting her to ask me for my Medi-Cal card so she could verify that the sticker was mine. Before she could say anything, I blurted out that I had forgotten my card. Strangely enough, I also didn't have any identification on me—because I had given them my girlfriend's name. After giving me the once-over, she shook her head in disgust and motioned for me to proceed into the waiting room. She knew I was a lying dog, but hey, lying dog or not, I *needed* an abortion.

My first abortion was pretty easy. A clerk called my fake name and put me in a small room with an examination table and stirrups. There was also a suction device, a mobile stool, and an instrument table for the doctor. I was given general anesthesia and slept through the fifteen-minute procedure. After I woke up, I rested for another hour, and then walked to the bus stop for my ride home. Except for feeling a little groggy, I was in an upbeat mood. I was scot-free and ready to resume having a good old time.

If I was supposed to come away from that experience feeling remorseful and depressed, it was completely lost on me. I didn't learn a thing. I picked up right where I left off and continued to have promiscuous sex with numerous partners. Two nights after the abortion, I went back to my favorite hangout, the Red Onion, a trendy Mexican restaurant and pick-up bar on Wilshire Boulevard just a couple of blocks down the street from my apartment. The Onion had a huge bar and a modest nine-by-twelve-foot parquet dance floor where I spent many wild nights discoing to a steady diet of Donna Summer's "Last Dance" and Gloria Gaynor's "I Will Survive." It was situated on the ground floor of an office tower and faced out onto a large courtyard where my friends and I used to sneak joints between heavy doses of margaritas and nachos. On weekdays, we could hit on guys who poured in from the office towers along Wilshire and on weekend nights, we mixed with the locals.

Whomever it was I was sleeping with at the time, I was doing it without birth control and managed to get away with it for six months before I got pregnant again in 1978. This time, I went down to the county welfare office myself. Welfare would pay me immediately if I produced a doctor's note saying I was pregnant. Going on the county allowed me to quit my job at the Fotomat store, which paid $90 a week, and live on the county for three months until I had my abortion. Free money. What a deal. I got $465 a month in aid from AFDC welfare and $80 in federal government food stamps. While this was awfully nice at the time, the real money was in doing the thing I mentioned on Oprah's show—illegally selling Medi-Cal stickers.

I began to study the market like a Wall Street stock pro, and I found that I could pick up an extra $100 to $400 a month on the side by selling off my surplus stickers to friends and acquaintances. When Medi-Cal issued me a card with the requisite eight stickers, I had to sell them fast because all of the stickers expired after one month. I had no intention of using any of them except when the time came to get an abortion. I soon became known as one of the "queenpins" of the Medi-Cal sticker black market.

Finding "clients" to buy my black market stickers was a cinch. Some were unemployment recipients who didn't want to apply for Medi-Cal because they were too lazy to ask their doctor for a pregnancy verification letter. Then they would have to head down to the county welfare office to fill out the nightmarish Medi-Cal paperwork, which was meant for the likes of a tax specialist. If they had an under-the-table job, it required getting a day off from work, which wasn't always easy to do.

My other customers were regular working folks, low-wage earners who were ineligible for Medi-Cal because they were employed. However, their company wasn't providing them any insurance and buying private insurance was beyond their means. Some had insurance plans that excluded eye exams, dental care, and, explicitly, abortions. I even sold stickers to some women who could have gotten an abortion on their insurance, but they were too embarrassed to have that procedure reported on their medical records. Well—for me, this all meant money in the bank.

Because I partied and clubbed around town, I had no trouble finding men and women in need of my services. I even had a roommate at the time who had a job at an accounting firm, so she referred co-workers who didn't have medical or dental insurance. She'd keep her ears open for prospects and bring home the cash. Then I'd give my roommate my Medi-Cal card to pass along to the client, and that person would go to the clinic posing as me. Since I sent people to places that were known for not requiring identification, this prevented any hassles. For others, I would simply give them a single sticker I had cut out from my card. Most doctors accepted them as long as the sticker was not peeled away. I usually made the exchange at my apartment or the Red Onion. I don't think the sticker black market was widespread, but there was enough competition out there to keep prices down.

Most of my business came from word of mouth. I'd be hanging out at the Red Onion or in Venice Beach and get introduced to a customer through an acquaintance. My boyfriends called when a pal needed a sticker for his pregnant girlfriend. I was never very worried about getting caught because I was careful about whom I was selling them to. Besides, I'd already visited the slammer once as a teenager, and going there again didn't intimidate me one bit.

For me, it was a great side business. On those few occasions I found girls who were four months pregnant and up, I made bank because they were facing an abortion bill ranging from $1,500 to $2,000 out of pocket. Suddenly, my Medi-Cal sticker for $400 looked terrific. But most of the deals I cut were small-time: $50 for a dental visit or an eye checkup, or $200 for a first-trimester abortion. In a good month, I could sell five stickers and make anywhere from $400 to $800.

My second abortion was scheduled for the same clinic

where my first one took place. This time I had my own sticker and the lady at the desk remembered me. She said: "I know you. You were just in here six months ago and didn't have any ID. I knew you were pretending to be someone else." I was speechless. I gave her the sticker, and she shot me another nasty look. Then she said: "Don't you ever think about taking the pill?" I didn't back down. I muttered back, "Well, if I took something you'd be out of a job wouldn't you?" I waited for a response but she didn't say a word.

Sitting in the waiting room, I thought about the birth control, or lack thereof, that I practiced. I had tried taking the pill after my first abortion but I got careless and kept missing days. Foams were inconvenient and the guys didn't like condoms because they claimed they couldn't feel anything. None of my girlfriends were practicing birth control either because the worst-case scenario in those days was getting either an abortion to deal with an unwanted pregnancy or a prescription to take care of a nasty venereal disease. I knew about the rhythm method and tried to practice that, obviously without much success. I was so ignorant about my body I didn't even know what an ovulation cycle was. If I had, I would have tried to identify my fertile time of the month and avoid having sex then.

Finally, they called my name, led me into the examination room, and put me out again.

I went right back to being sexually active after my second abortion, so when my period didn't come a few months later, I panicked—"Oh no, I'm pregnant again." It was late 1978 and my third pregnancy in a little more than a year. I headed down to the welfare office once more and signed up for benefits. This time, I didn't want to get any grief from the woman at the Crenshaw clinic, so a couple of months later I made an appointment at a clinic located in a fancy medical building on Wilshire Boulevard near my apartment. It was a world away from Crenshaw. The waiting room chairs were plush and on the walls of the reception area hung breezy paintings of Redwood forests and rocky coastlines. All the office workers and nurses were white. At the Crenshaw clinic, the staff and patients were black, except for the doctors, who were mostly white.

When I arrived, I should have sensed this clinic was trouble because everybody acted rude to me. The woman at the desk just tossed me a clipboard and ordered me to fill out the medical forms. She kept asking, "Where's the Medi-Cal sticker?" I knew the color of my skin had something to do with that shabby treatment.

I didn't have to wait long to have the procedure. That was a relief because being so close to home, I was worried I might run into a friend. But once I was under the doctor's care, it turned into one of the longest and most painful experiences of my life. During my first two abortions, I made sure the doctors put me under. When I asked this doctor for a general anesthetic, he said they didn't do that here and if I wanted to be put to sleep, I should go back to the Crenshaw clinic.

I should have been more assertive, but I was feeling vulnerable and didn't know what I was in for, so I kept my mouth shut. The doctor was this big, fat, balding man with a moon-shaped face and tiny wire-rim glasses. I imagine he looked like my childhood vision of Dr. Frankenstein. I got up on the table and slid my legs into the stirrups. I was up on my elbows trying to watch everything he did. He inserted a vacuum device inside my body and boy did it hurt. I felt his hands, too. The pain got so bad I started to complain.

"Shut up," he said.

I protested again, and he said, "You'd better shut up or I'm going to stop right where I am."

When I asked for some anesthesia, once again he barked back, "I told you we *don't* do that here." I left that "uptown" clinic hating that doctor more than any white racist I had ever known. I thought he was a red-necked bigot whose goal in life was to inflict pain on black women who came there for abortions.

While that nasty doctor had actually scared some sense into me, it wasn't enough to keep me from getting knocked up for a fourth time a year later. It was late 1979 and I had spent the past year living with a guy named Lou whom I had met through a girlfriend. We shared a one-bedroom apartment for $250 a month on Ardmore Street, two blocks north of Wilshire Boulevard. He was six foot four, played recreational basketball, and had a job pitching party tents for a catering company. I was off welfare and now working too, earning $150 a week in the circulation department of the *Los Angeles Times*. I made $7 an hour taking newspaper delivery complaints over the phone, which required me to be at work by six A.M. three days a week. On our days off together, Lou and I hung out at Venice Beach. I watched him play ball and then we'd find some friends and get high, usually on angel dust.

I wasn't in love with Lou when he got me pregnant. In fact, I was already thinking of splitting up with him. He was starting to experiment with more serious drugs, like smoking crack, and I wanted no part of that. When I told him about the pregnancy, he suggested a family planning clinic on Sixth Street and Westmoreland where a friend of his had taken a girlfriend to get an abortion.

That was all right by me. This clinic was close to home and I didn't want to face that woman at the Crenshaw clinic for a third time. And I had no intention of going back to see old Dr. Frankenstein. For this procedure, I paid with a Medi-Cal sticker and demanded that the doctor put me to sleep. The discomfort I felt was more psychological than physical. I knew who the father was this time and that made going through with it more difficult. This baby inside of me wasn't so anonymous. As I sat in the waiting room with Lou, I imagined what a child by us could look like and shivered with anxiety. I also thought about my previous procedure and that gestapo doctor. When my name was called, I let go of Lou's hand, got up, and thought to myself, "After today, I'm not doing this anymore." It was my fourth time through those doors, and by god my last.

Well, lo and behold, a few months later, in February 1980, I was pregnant for a fifth time. I decided I was going to have this baby, but I didn't tell Lou because he wasn't the father. This child belonged to a man named Jerry, a student at Los Angeles City College, where I had begun taking classes the previous fall.

Jerry was going through a lot of emotional problems. His stepdad had recently died, and we became very close talking over coffee about his feelings of loss. We were taking a broadcasting and an art course together. Lou was either working or getting high somewhere when I saw Jerry during school hours. After class, we'd go to my girlfriend's house, where we had sex a few times.

Jerry was much different from Lou. He wanted to get a college degree, while Lou was consumed with free-basing cocaine. Lou was turning into a zombie before my very eyes. He expressed neither highs nor lows, and lost all interest in sex.

Between my studies and my job at the *Times*, it was impossible to keep pace with Lou's partying. When I first started my job, my boss liked me and talked about promoting me into a different department. I was even moved out to the front counter because I had a nice voice and was good with people.

It was here that I got my first taste of backlash from my jealous friends. I discovered being a good employee and playing it by the book qualified me as a "house nigger"— someone who kissed a white man's butt to get a cushy job. My friends called my ethnicity into question, teasing me about becoming "one of them." It was always "them" and "us." So I stopped being polite to customers and started looking down on management. There was a lot of peer pressure from the other blacks not to join the system, and I backed off the track because I was more worried about losing my friends than getting a promotion.

Being pregnant made matters even worse. I was exhausted and sick all the time, and getting up for work in the morning became an impossible task. I began losing patience with the newspaper customers and getting reprimands from my boss for being late. He gave me a lot of chances. My job performance suffered and before they could fire me, I quit and went back to living on the county.

I moved out on Lou and found another apartment on Ardmore Street. It had a fireplace, Jacuzzi, pool, and a subterranean garage. I felt like I was Zsa Zsa Gabor. The rent was $285 a month. My budget would be tight, but I decided to move in. I could always fall back on the black market for Medi-Cal stickers.

One day I got a call from my social worker from the welfare office and she said she wanted to come by to see where I was living. I freaked. I was still being evaluated for benefits and if she saw I could afford a nice apartment, she might start to wonder if I was taking money under the table. She could reduce my aid or cut me off entirely. About half an hour before she was supposed to arrive, she called to cancel the appointment; she wanted to go to lunch with a girlfriend and asked me to cover for her in case anyone from the county inquired. I was thrilled. I said, "Okay, honey, you have yourself a fine lunch!"

By now I was a pro at working the system. Once my welfare was squared away, my next move was to find a job that paid $100 a week under the table. By moving out on Lou, I had in effect more than doubled my rent from the $125 a month I was paying while living with him. Though I was pregnant and back on welfare again, I had no desire to slow down my lifestyle. I liked going out with friends and enjoyed buying a new outfit from time to time. So I hopped on the bus and headed south toward Crenshaw. There were a lot of small businesses there that I had heard paid people off the books. Many of those businesses couldn't afford to pay minimum wage along with Social Security, unemployment, Workers' Compensation, and disability taxes. I'd gladly give them thirty-five hours a week of my time for $100 cash. That was more than enough to supplement my welfare check and food stamps.

I found a job at a small advertising agency run by three young Christian guys—Kenneth, Prince, and Gerald. I was fascinated by them. They were confident and optimistic, and possessed an entrepreneurial drive. Their energy was contagious, and they were impressed that I was taking college courses and had held a job at the *Times.* I accepted the job, but they would not pay me under the table. So I kept withholding my Social Security number from them to keep my name from going on the books.

I think the only reason they didn't fire me was because they saw me as their reclamation project. They kept promising me I was going to be saved by Jesus Christ. I decided to try a little shock treatment on them. I told them some stories about my past escapades and admitted to them I liked partying and going out with guys. They had answers straight from the Bible for every immoral thing I gabbed about, from casual sex to smoking pot. For instance, when I argued there was nothing wrong with getting high once in a while, they showed me where it says in the Bible that your body is the Temple of God and you should treat it with respect. I just smiled and shook my head. I was as intimidated as a mouse in a pantry.

That job lasted only a few months. The two secrets I kept from the guys were that I was pregnant and on welfare. They continued to pressure me for my Social Security number for their payroll records, and I quit in August when I was six months' pregnant.

By this time, my personal life was in shambles. That summer, I let Lou move back into my apartment because he had lost his lease after I left the old place and he was living on the street. I soon discovered Lou was consumed by drugs. Jerry broke up with me before he even learned I was pregnant, so I didn't see him the entire time I was carrying his daughter. He was four years younger than I was and got frustrated because I wasn't serious about him and wouldn't leave Lou. I eventually told him about the baby, but he was convinced I had gotten pregnant by Lou. I wasn't up to arguing about it with him, so I let it be. That fall, he moved away to San Francisco to finish up his schooling.

Going through the pregnancy alone was a huge mistake. I was skipping my prenatal checkups and spending most of my time partying with friends in Venice. I was still into drugs, angel dust mostly, although I had curtailed my use substantially after getting pregnant. One reason was because I was feeling sick all the time. My body was bloated and my ankles and hands were swollen. One of my girlfriends warned me, "Girl, you're looking awful! You gotta go to the doctor."

It was about this time that I finally told my parents I was living on the county. My mother, as usual, didn't say anything. My father was disgusted with me and called me a disgrace to the Irby family name. He said I was the first person in the family ever to go on welfare. One day on the phone, he gave me a stern lecture: "We all worked too hard for too long for one of us to go and do that."

I even heard from some of my relatives in South Carolina. One aunt called and complained, "We sure never went on welfare, Larstella! How could you? We all thought you were going to be the one who was going to make it." I had no idea that they had that much confidence in me and that I had let them all down.

Even my uncle Chuck from Sacramento stopped speaking to me. He had put me up for a few months when I moved to California in 1976. Years later, after I was off welfare, I found out he was sick with lung cancer. I called him and he said, "What are you calling for?"

I said, "I'm calling to see how you're doing 'cause my dad told me you had cancer."

He said, "So."

I said, "I just wanted to make sure you were all right. You know, you're my favorite uncle."

He said, "Oh, I figured you was calling to see if I could send you some money."

I said, "I'm not calling for that, but if you have some you can send it." I was just joking but he hung up.

During the fall of 1980, I kicked Lou out for good. He drifted away and I didn't see him again until years later. I was up in the old neighborhood visiting an advertising client for my magazine and I spotted him standing on the corner of Normandie Avenue and Fifth Street. He was pushing a shopping cart, homeless. I didn't recognize him at first, but he has always had wonderful, sleepy eyes with long eyelashes. I looked at him and said, "Oh my God, it's you—Lou!" I tried to get his attention, but he didn't appear to recognize me, so I moved on.

After Lou was out of my life, I started dating this new guy named James, whom I had met at the beach. One September afternoon, we were sitting around my apartment and talking about whether I should go back home to Mount Holly, New Jersey, after I had my baby. My parents had said I could come home and they would help me out. Looking back, that would have been the smartest thing to do. Then again, making wise choices was not my forte.

"C'mon," James said. "We're going for a drive."

We took a ride up Doheny Hill, which is just above the

world-famous HOLLYWOOD sign. It was a perfect fall day and we could see clear down to the Pacific Ocean, even as far out as Catalina Island, twenty miles offshore. While I was staring at the horizon and contemplating life back in Mount Holly, James asked, "Do you really want to leave all this?" I said, "No way, I love it here. I love Hollywood." It was exotic and I was enjoying life. New Jersey was no comparison.

Moving back in with my parents would have meant following their rules and possibly getting a full-time job. Forget that—I had no desire to go back to work. I also had done some homework on the welfare scene back in Jersey, and it was not good news. I actually made a call to find out how much that state paid out to welfare mothers, and it was a paltry $170 a month. I was getting $465 in LA, plus food stamps, which was enough to rent my one-bedroom apartment with a Jacuzzi just steps from my front door. "What a setup," I thought to myself. "I get my welfare, my food stamps, and medical stickers. This ain't too bad. I could go through life like this well into my twilight years!"

4

ANGEL ON MY SHOULDER

On October 17, 1980, one month before my baby was due, I woke up feeling really sick. My body felt like it was going to explode and I had a pounding headache. A girlfriend had once told me if your body is swelling, you probably have toxemia, an illness caused by toxins invading the blood from an infection. Today it's called preeclampsia.

I had an appointment later in the day with my doctor, but I called to see if he could take me that morning. "Oh, don't worry about it," he said. "I'll see you in the afternoon."

I was a real pain-in-the-ass patient and I'm not sure my doctor enjoyed treating someone like me. I was seeing him because he had privileges at Cedars-Sinai, one of the best private hospitals in the world. It's where all the movie stars went to have their kids, so I knew it was good. At the time, it was my understanding that Cedars didn't accept Medi-Cal insurance unless your doctor had access to the facilities. When the time came to deliver this child, I wanted the best; I didn't care that I was a Medi-Cal patient.

After I hung up with my doctor, my headache got worse. I

called him back and he finally said to come in. His office was forty-five minutes away by bus. Somehow, I hobbled to the bus stop, despite the fact that my body felt like it might explode.

I took the bus west on Wilshire and then transferred to a second bus to go south on Crenshaw. After transferring to a third bus, I just kind of collapsed in my seat. The driver took one look at me and said, "Are you all right?" I groaned, "No, I'm so sick." He could see I was pregnant so he pulled over and dialed 911. When he returned, he said I was going to be put in an ambulance and taken to the nearest hospital.

I was rushed by ambulance to Brotman Medical Center, where the emergency room doctors took one look at me and said, "We don't do preemies. You're about to have this baby and you're going to blow up." They were freaking out. The fluid inside my body was building up and was endangering my health and the health of my baby. I was thinking, "They don't know what to do with me here even though I'm gonna die and my baby's gonna die."

I was wheeled back outside on a gurney, put in an ambulance, and transferred to UCLA Medical Center. As the sirens blared, all I could think about was how much money this was going to cost me since ambulance rides weren't covered under Medi-Cal.

The paramedics wheeled me into the emergency room and I was immediately surrounded by three doctors. What struck me was how young and caring they were. Ironically, they were all white guys, and I had already experienced a stormy childhood with white people. When they took me into the delivery room, things started to sink in. These doctors were going to deliver my baby and they didn't care the least bit about what color I was. Right before they put me under, one of them said to me: "We're on your side and we're going to deliver your child for you today." Then I heard an older doctor say to a younger one, "This is where you're going to cut." I found out later that the doctor who did the surgery performed his very first cesarean on me.

Hours later, I woke up exhausted, but I found out my little girl was okay. She weighed five pounds and was very healthy despite being three weeks premature. I named her Angel because I wanted a "good kid" and I thought that name would start her off on the right path. They kept Angel in the hospital a week for observation, and they were stuck with me too because I refused to leave without my baby. What was I going to do? I didn't have a car and I was not about to take a bus from my home in mid-Wilshire all the way across town to UCLA to pick up my daughter. It was a long and lonely week. No one in my family could afford to fly out to see me, and I had only one visitor, Kenneth, one of the born-again Christian guys I used to work for at the advertising agency. If it weren't for the kind nurses, I would have had a miserable time. As it was, I ate, slept, and breast-fed Angel. Eventually, I reached a neighbor who was able to come and give us both a ride home.

For the next six weeks, I spent most of my time resting in bed with Angel, thinking about what changes I needed to make in my life. Number one on my list was quitting hard drugs. Because I feared some of my friends might ostracize me, I was reluctant to quit smoking pot. Slowing down wasn't too difficult since my routine at this point was getting up to make some soup and coming back to bed to breast-feed Angel. My neighbor Suzy ran errands for us, but after a few weeks, I was able to bundle up Angel, put her in a stroller, and walk to a corner minimart to buy diapers, milk, and food using my food stamps.

When the lease expired on the Ardmore place, the landlord raised the rent $30 a month on my one-bedroom. That made a big difference because that particular year welfare didn't give us a cost of living raise. With two mouths to feed, I was being squeezed dry. Since I wasn't out socializing as much, the Medi-Cal sticker market was drying up. Besides, I needed most of the stickers for myself and Angel. So I started looking for another place to live.

THE BEST LITTLE WELFARE HOUSE OFF WILSHIRE

I had a girlfriend named Leona who was looking for an apartment with her sister Brenda. We got together and rented a three-bedroom place, bringing in two other single mothers, Janet and Penny, to share the expenses. We gave one mom the den and the other a bedroom. I had a bedroom with Angel and the two sisters shared a third bedroom with Brenda's daughter. Our new home was in an old brick building on Mariposa Street near Wilshire Boulevard, just two blocks from my one-bedroom on Ardmore. Gone were the Jacuzzi, fireplace, and subterranean garage, but you couldn't beat the price: $550 for three bedrooms and a den, and we split the cost five ways.

One of my roommates worked and the other three were welfare moms. Brenda detested housework and we were always picking up after her and her daughter, who was about two years older than Angel. Janet was a free spirit living the kind of life I used to live. Her daughter spent much of the time with her grandmother while Janet would go out and date different guys. There was one rule of the house no one broke: no men were allowed to stay overnight. We didn't want the kids seeing men running in and out. The third welfare mom's name was Penny, a sweet and generous soul who was always ready to lend a hand and help out around the house.

Leona was the only one who had a job and who didn't have a

child. She worked in payroll for an accounting office. In my eyes, she made really good money, $350 to $400 a week. But she had a history of holding a job for eight months or so and then quitting to collect unemployment. When she got back in the mood, she'd get another job, then take another extended vacation. She'd sleep in and then spend the day watching game shows and the soaps with the rest of us. We loved *Hollywood Squares* and *All My Children*. At night, Leona would head out to party.

Leona and Brenda used to have problems with Brenda's social worker because welfare didn't like Brenda living with another family member. They feared Leona might be supporting her younger sister and that Brenda might share some of her food stamp benefits with Leona. The sisters even had to keep their food separated in the refrigerator in case of an impromptu visit by the social worker.

In my opinion, this is a major flaw in the welfare system. I believe families should be able to stay together until the person on welfare can get back on her feet. If you split up people like Leona and Brenda, they're both going to struggle and that can lead to more government dependency. If welfare officials don't want people to cheat, they can solve the problem by allowing recipients to spend the money on something other than basic necessities. What's the problem with having a working sister pay the rent while the other uses the money to fix her teeth or buy some nice clothes so she can go job hunting? If we're going to have welfare, I think we should eliminate many of the rules and regulations and simply restrict the length of time someone can receive it. That would certainly eliminate the need for an army of pit bull watchdogs and most of the red tape while still providing the aid.

Living with four children and four adult women didn't offer much privacy. On the other hand, it was a good sharing situation. We did grocery shopping together at the local Vons supermarket, pooled our food stamps, and shared the cooking. While we were friends and had our family squabbles, we also led independent lives.

There was a lot of drug dealing and prostitution going on in our neighborhood. Across the street and down one block, there was a decrepit two-story hotel that was an active whorehouse. I used to see a lot of trashy-looking girls coming and going from the hotel, usually with businessmen on their arms. Their eye liner was always overdone and the fire-engine-red lipstick applied unevenly. Their usual wardrobe consisted of hot pants, high heels, tight miniskirts, and leotards. The johns would come over from the big corporations that were headquartered along Wilshire, so you knew they had some money to spend. Further up my street and closer to Third Avenue, there was usually a male drug dealer working the corner with pockets full of cocaine, PCP, and marijuana.

In March 1981, when Angel was five months old, I returned to Los Angeles City College after having dropped out the previous spring because of my pregnancy. I took classes that interested me, like journalism, advertising, and art. I had attended classes on and off since 1976 and discovered I was just a few credits shy of a community college degree. For the first time in my life, I actually felt I might be capable of doing something with my education, like getting a full-time job after graduation. Having Angel and desiring a decent life for her pushed me into action. I often brought her along with me to class, where she'd nap in her baby seat or drink apple juice from a bottle. Most of the time, she was really good, yet even when she'd cry, the other students and professors rarely gave me a hard time.

All this time, Kenneth, Gerald, and Prince never gave up on me. When I told them I had returned to school, it inspired them to keep on me about becoming a Christian. They often called to see if I would join them for church, so one Sunday during that spring I finally relented and attended services with them at the Crenshaw Christian Center.

The parish hall, located at Ninety-sixth Street and Crenshaw Boulevard in Inglewood, was decorated with sparkling
white interior walls and a magnificent red carpet. The clergy
and choir wore bold purple robes and sang to sweet Christian
music backed by a powerful pipe organ. Fresh flowers adorned
the altar, amplifying the festive atmosphere. I really didn't
know what to expect, but the beauty, the pageantry, and the
positive energy flowing through that building sent chills
through my body. In the congregation, there were middle-
class blacks who were doing well professionally and enjoying
the time spent with their families. It was refreshing to see a
group of hardworking black people compared to the group I
was hanging out with. My roommates seemed to be going
through life one day at a time, and these people had goals.

So I returned and made some new friends, including a
young married couple, a homemaker named Paula and her
insurance salesman husband, Gerald. After church one Sunday, they invited me to their house for dinner. They lived in a
nice tract home in a beautiful Inglewood neighborhood with
manicured lawns and landscaped gardens. The streets were
lined with palm trees and children played ball outdoors and
rode bicycles up and down the sidewalks. I remember the day
because it was the first time I had been in a married couple's
home since moving to Los Angeles. Over a cup of coffee, Paula
told me she was a stay-at-home mom. I smiled and said, "You
kidding, right?" She wasn't, and at that moment I realized I
had lost sight of this part of the world. I had never set foot in a
middle-class black neighborhood filled with married couples
and their children living in three-bedroom homes. Because it
was so far outside my universe, I had never envisioned myself
taking that path.

In 1982 I was still jobless, living off welfare, and partying
occasionally with the old crowd from Venice. The difference
was I was going to church on a regular basis. Pastor Fred Price
was a very articulate black man who spoke often of the

future. Sometimes I felt his sermons were directed at the possibilities of my own future. He became the most influential person in my life.

One Sunday he talked about his children and how important it was to set a good example for them. I felt I could be spending more quality time with Angel, yet I was still leading what Reverend Price would call "the best bad life." Then he sermonized about "a best good life," and I thought, "Why not give that one a try?"

First, I vowed to get all those nasty men out of my life and abstain from sex until I got married. Pastor Price preached "no sex before marriage" as an absolute standard and said we all had the power to make that decision. I decided to heed his words and start being a proper role model for my daughter.

My roommates gave me a hard time about my new resolutions. Instead of flirting with the guys playing basketball at Venice Beach, I'd go jogging in the morning or roller skating along the Venice boardwalk, which runs alongside the beach. I quit eating junk food and resisted the men who made passes at me. I decided to use sex as a power play: "I'm waiting until my Prince Charming comes along and asks me to marry him," I'd tell them.

I also stopped smoking pot. In the back of my mind, I suspected my drug use might have had something to do with why Angel was a month premature and why my health had deteriorated during the pregnancy. While convalescing after her birth, I had beaten myself up for almost jeopardizing the life of my daughter. I was thankful we had both survived the delivery.

Furthering my education was another part of my plan. In the fall of 1982, I enrolled at Woodbury University, which occupied a large office building on Wilshire Boulevard. I applied for some grants and loans to study marketing. Two years earlier, my circulation boss at the *Los Angeles Times* said he thought I had the potential to work in the paper's marketing department, but I walked away from that opportunity. Now I was ready to give it another try.

I also took a vow of honesty, so to speak. For years, I had prided myself on my ability to abuse and exploit the welfare system. Every month, they sent out CA-7 forms asking the same five questions:

- Did you open a bank account?
- Are you going to school?
- Did you earn any outside income over $25?
- Did you get married?
- Did you get a roommate?

I always knew to check off the "no" box for each item to avoid hassles, but this time, being a churchgoer, I checked off the box saying "yes," I was in school. The county responded by stopping my check and threatening to sue me for back payments.

I went downtown to the county welfare office and met with my social worker. It was a different place this time. In the past, I'd make an appointment on the same day as one of my friends and we'd make a day of it: after meeting with our social workers, we'd grab lunch at a nearby hamburger stand and then head over to the famous Olvera Street neighborhood for a margarita. At this appointment, I took one look around the building and realized my time as a welfare hustler was expiring. I was surrounded by sullen faces and felt I didn't have anything in common with them anymore.

After an hour's wait and another hour for my social worker to check the regulations, I was informed that it was all right to receive a California state grant for college and AFDC welfare at the same time. That was great news because I planned on using part of the loan to buy a moped for transportation. The bus system in Los Angeles was too unreliable and I wanted to get to class on time. After I purchased it, I put a toddler seat on the back for Angel and got her a little helmet.

Of all the changes in my life, getting off welfare was the toughest. I promised myself that I would stop by the time I earned my bachelor's degree from Woodbury in June 1983. But even after graduation, I remained dependent on those government checks. I even went out looking for another job that paid under the table. To me, welfare was still an entitlement and discarding it would be like parting with one of my civil liberties.

QUITTING THE COUNTY

One Sunday in the summer of 1983, I was sitting in church listening to one of Pastor Price's sermons on welfare, a subject that obviously hit very close to home. He looked out over the congregation, some four thousand people, and he bellowed, "What are you doing living on welfare!"

If ever there was a time when I thought my skin turned white with fear, that was the moment. I could have sworn Pastor Price was speaking directly to me. Then he said, "The government is not your source. God is your source. He's the one who takes care of you. You do not depend on the government!" He said it emphatically. He was absolute and almost angry.

Pastor Price looked in my direction, and I began to cower. "Oh dear," I said to myself. "Who told him I was on the county?" On the way home in a friend's car, I sat there thinking, "How did he know?" It hit me hard. I thought about his words, "God is your source," and I never let up on that. When I got back to my apartment, I sat down on the couch and made my decision right there. There were now five kids living in our apartment and no husbands, and I just stood up and hollered: *"I'm quitting the county!"*

My roommates scoffed at me. They didn't believe it. A lot had changed since we moved in together. Leona, who I think was bothered that I might do something with my life, now had a baby and was supported by welfare. Janet was still whining about the rule that men couldn't sleep over. Brenda was going to church with me and so was Leona. The difference was when we got home, Brenda and I wanted to talk about the Bible and Leona wanted us to put it away. Leona was a real possessive person and she didn't like my new Christian friends.

I could have predicted everyone's reaction to my news. Leona asked how I was going to pay the rent. Janet was freaking out. Brenda didn't seem to care. Only Penny, who was so passive and sweet, was supportive. She never had an unkind word or pessimistic viewpoint—just the type of person you need around when you're about to take a giant risk.

The next day, I called my social worker and told her to stop mailing me my welfare checks. She told me to put it in writing. So with a pen and paper, I wrote the department a note instructing them to take me off the rolls. I quoted Pastor Price: "God is my source. He's going to take care of me."

When my social worker received my letter, she called me up and said skeptically, "Yeah right, you're going off welfare? How you gonna eat?" She then sent me two more checks, figuring I didn't mean what I had said. Only after I stopped filling out my monthly CA-7 forms did the county finally cut me off.

I had no idea what was in store for me next.

5

TAKING THE MORAL
HIGH GROUND

When I got off welfare, being poor wasn't something new to me. While I never went hungry during my childhood, I knew what it was like to get by on a tight budget. In those first weeks after my welfare check stopped arriving in the mail and a $200 loan from my mother was all spent, I drew on these early lessons to get by.

During my youth, we moved around a lot and I was used to doing things on my own. This contributed to my independent demeanor and put me at odds with my mother, Doris. When my father, James, was transferred to an Air Force base in Peru, Indiana, in 1960, the house we lived in had a huge basement. I used to hide down there from my mother when I got in trouble. As the middle of five children, it was hard for me to find my place in the family. My oldest sister Avis was the firstborn and got favored treatment from my mother, and they developed a close relationship over the years. I was envious of their connection and frequently fought with both of them, even as a little girl.

I remember once when I started playing with a heating

grate on the kitchen floor. Mother must have told me a hundred times to stay away from it. But I was a curious sort, so one day when she wasn't home, I pulled up the grate with a friend to peek inside. Avis saw me do it and squealed on me. As my mother went outside to get a switch off a tree, I ran down to the basement to hide. I stayed there for over an hour and when I eventually reappeared, she gave me quite a whipping.

Mother—and she always insisted we call her "Mother"— believed in giving us a good spanking when we had it coming to us, even if she was little—no more than five foot one and ninety-five pounds. She wore a size 2 dress. Mother was not an affectionate person, so there was never any hugging and kissing or affirming of good behavior. In fact, to this day, I cannot remember my mother and father making any type of love gesture toward one another. They were very quiet and private people. You know how parents sometimes fight but the kids also know they love each other? Our parents never fought in front of us, nor was there any touching. To tell you the truth, I never thought about it much, but I think it's part of the reason why today I have to remind myself to go hug my husband and my kids.

Showing affection is something that does not come naturally to me. Maybe that's why people thought I was cold and callous growing up. I didn't care deeply about any of my old boyfriends. I certainly never thought about getting married and having kids. In fact, I convinced myself I'd do the opposite.

My mother and father grew up in Greenville, South Carolina, raised under the heavy hand of Jim Crow. While their neighborhood was segregated from the white community, there wasn't the kind of antagonism between whites and blacks as in other parts of the South. Blacks did have to attend separate churches, schools, and restaurants, and in the few integrated establishments, blacks were relegated to second-class status. They were required to enter through back doors of restaurants and sit in the back of buses. My father recalled that blacks could go to only one theater in town, ironically named the Liberty. He could sit only in the balcony, and that's where he met my mom. He spotted her during a Gregory Peck movie and asked one of my mother's sisters if he could sit next to her.

Dad said the most serious racist incident he was ever involved in came when he got punched in the face by a white man. He was still a teenager and had taken a bus to Anderson, South Carolina, to visit some relatives. Outside the terminal, he went for a walk to find something to eat and passed by three white men. For no reason, one of them slugged him in the jaw. His mouth was cut but he didn't retaliate. He said it wouldn't have been to any benefit if he had struck back. Besides, he didn't have trouble like that in Greenville.

I can't recall my father ever hitting me. He was strict, and while my other brothers and sisters didn't always get along with him, he took a special liking to me. He always said I was a talker. "Larstella, let me tell you something—talkers *rule* the world!" My dad was always fascinated by my being able to articulate an idea, and he encouraged me with stories about great leaders like Napoléon, Harriet Tubman, and Frederick Douglass. I might spend the week daydreaming about being a great general or a legendary abolitionist, and then brag to my brothers and sisters that dad said there were a certain percentage of people who become leaders and that I could be one someday. So I'd tell them, "I'm going to be on top," and my mother would say, "Well, you do have a big mouth!" I loved my dad for telling me I was a terrific talker because everyone else said I talked too much. Some still say I do.

But if talkers ruled the world, and I was a good talker, I wanted to make the most of it. For these were the people who were well-off, had nice clothes, fancy cars, and big houses.

Now I didn't know anything about how people accumulated things, or any of the different means of making it rich, but I simply believed if some people could make a lot of money, I could too! I was going to do it someday.

In 1962, my father was transferred to McGuire Air Force Base in Mount Holly, New Jersey. Mount Holly was a white town and the base had to find him a house because nobody in the surrounding neighborhoods wanted a black family living next door, especially a large one. I could tell our neighbors despised us, which was ironic, since Harriet Tubman and the Underground Railroad had come that way during the Civil War. When my father and mother went to look at the house we eventually bought, a woman came over and scolded the real estate agent: "If you want those people living next to you, why don't you show them a home in your neighborhood?" she said.

The brick house we lived in was a thousand square feet and contained three bedrooms and one bath. It was a tight fit for a family of seven. When we arrived, we were one of the first black families to move into the neighborhood, and during the three years we were there, the white families gradually moved away. Today it's totally black.

I started kindergarten at Fowell Elementary School in Mount Holly, and I don't recall ever seeing any black teachers there. The white teachers never bothered to call me Larstella. Usually, it was just plain Stella.

School was an uninspiring place and I never did homework. All through my education I never read a book and as a result, I still have trouble reading today. I went through school getting B's and C's and always thought I was a good student and could retain what the teachers repeated in class, but most of the time I was just making wild guesses. Fortunately, I didn't do all that badly. I never failed anything, which doesn't say much for our educational system.

When I raised my hand, the teachers rarely called on me no matter how high I stretched my arm. I didn't have any friends, nor did I talk or play with any of the white kids. I was just always by myself. Most of the other kids were blond and blue-eyed and it was strange for me because those kids seemed "whiter" in Mount Holly than they were in Indiana. In Indiana, my white friends played with me on the teeter-totter and the swing. In Mount Holly I was alone.

That was okay by me because I daydreamed a lot and wrote down what I was thinking. I liked to imagine what life would be like if it was like what I saw on television. I loved old movies where the girls had real smooth faces and big beautiful eyes and smoked those long cigarettes. The women always had gorgeous blond hair, were thin, and wore long flowing dresses. Except for the blond hair, I figured I could look glamorous and be an actress someday. It never occurred to me that these white celebrities were the same kinds of white people I went to school with. There was something different about those television icons and somehow they made it appear accessible.

But I knew I was different, and it didn't help matters that my mother made no effort to make us all fit in. She'd put big ol' pigtails in my hair when all the white girls were wearing their hair straight. I would always tell her I wanted my hair out but she made Avis, and Vera, and me wear pigtails way on top of our heads. That's probably why I idolized Angela Davis when I was older. It wasn't the politics so much as the fact that she was a tough and strong black woman who got to wear her hair out. Years later, I had an afro that made me look like a sun goddess.

Things weren't any better around my neighborhood be-cause the white kids avoided me there, too. One day, I was outside and I waved at a little girl across the street. I walked up to her and the first words out of her mouth were, "I can't play with you 'cause you're a nigger." I could tell she didn't even understand what she was saying, and neither did I. I went home and asked my mother what a "nigger" meant. I don't think she responded. My parents never talked to us about issues, yet this was when the civil rights movement was just starting to heat up all over the South.

Kids are always going to ask questions and the response they receive will sometimes determine how they perceive things in their future. When I was much older I went to a church that was almost all white, and a little girl sitting in the pew in front of me started rubbing me to see if my black would come off. She figured, "Wow, how come she's dark chocolate. I wonder if it comes off?" That's okay. Kids just need to know people come in all different shapes, sizes, and colors, but what really counts is what goes on beneath the veneer.

My parents didn't even talk about President John F. Kennedy after he was assassinated. All I know is that when he died what upset me the most was that I had had a big party planned for my seventh birthday and President Kennedy ruined it. Everybody was depressed about him but I didn't care. My birthday was messed up every year because it was too close to Thanksgiving, Christmas, and John Kennedy's assassination.

Despite the problems in Mount Holly, my father felt very comfortable there because he came from real poverty. He was the firstborn from a family of nine that lived in a *three-room* house in Greenville, South Carolina. Warreno Irby is my grandmother, and she's dirt poor. Still, she taught me more about morality and pride than any person I've ever known.

Grandma Warreno was a big woman, five-foot-eight and 180 pounds. She got married at age fourteen and had my dad two years later. Over a twenty-one-year period, she had six sons and one daughter who died at age fourteen of a heart condition brought on by rheumatic fever. My grandmother never saw all six of her sons together until they held a reunion back in 1974. She raised them all in the same gray clapboard house where she still lives today at the age of eighty. Grandma's bedroom was in the front of the house, and her boys slept in the second room. The last room, overlooking the backyard, was the kitchen. Outside grandma's house there was a chicken coop and a garden where she grew potatoes, green beans, and collard greens. She used to love to cook— her favorites were ox tails, chitlins, chicken, and grits. The fresh vegetables came straight from her garden.

Grandma's house wasn't dirty, it was just ugly. When I was a little girl, I always used to complain about going to the bathroom because the toilet was outside, between her house and my great grandmother's house. It was a nasty and dank little outhouse that was filled with spiders and cobwebs. We took baths outside in a big, old, rusted metal tub with water from a nearby pump. I dreaded bathing there. I'd start trouble on purpose so I could leave and go to my aunt's house, where they had nice indoor plumbing. Not too long ago, the state health department made grandma install an indoor toilet and she was not happy about that at all. She was so set in her ways, and proud of her independence, that she didn't like anyone telling her what to do. I must admit, I think I probably have a little bit of grandma in me.

From the time I was five years old, our family summered in Greenville, and I hated it. The South seemed somehow wicked to me. I didn't even know why. I didn't know the history, but I just didn't like the long winding roads and the absence of streetlights and sidewalks. I didn't like people always saying hello to me. I was very private, even as a little girl. When people said "Hi," I thought they were getting in my way and I would say, "Get out of my business."

It was so hot down there that my mother dressed me in stupid little cotton dresses that went straight down over my hips. I looked like a character out of *The Little Rascals.* I always despised white clothes and soft pastels. I preferred dark colors—reds, purples, and blacks—and I picked them out myself. Before I could go outside, mother would spread Vaseline all over my legs and arms to keep my skin from drying up.

The other thing I hated about Greenville was that my grandma was poor and seemed content to live like that. One of her sons, Uncle Rufus, still lives with her today. We called him "Pie," a nickname that caught on when a little girl called him a "ninny pie" when he was just a baby. I never called him "uncle" because he was only about five years older than me. When I was little I used to ask my dad and Pie, "Why don't you get grandma a better house?" My family is kind of laid back and they figured if she liked it that way, no sense in changing it. I felt ashamed for her. I once said, "Grandma, how can you live like this when you could live like Elizabeth Taylor, if you *really* wanted!" (I obviously watched a lot of movies in those days.) Grandma looked around her home and said, "This is the best I'll ever have. Don't you judge my life. God has blessed me with a lot!"

It would take me years to comprehend what she was saying, but I'm not sure former president Lyndon Johnson and the other authors of the Great Society would know what she was getting at. When President Johnson vowed to end poverty with a series of welfare programs in the 1960s, he presumed the plight of the poor would be obliterated if government, and not individual incentive, provided the means to upgrade an individual's standard of living. What he didn't anticipate was that many of those who went on the welfare rolls would lose their self-initiative and never get off public assistance, a sad legacy that has been passed on to subsequent generations. Then there are other poor folks like my grandmother who had no need for handouts in the first place, despite being told otherwise by supposedly well-intentioned Democrats. She has gotten by on hard work, frugality, and faith, virtues that I believe make a society great.

In Greenville, I used to follow Pie around, who was always up to some kind of harmless mischief. He'd walk up the street and hang out in front of the liquor store, and I'd be right behind him. Grandma hated it when I went up there, and she used to come down there with a switch to get me.

I was seven at the time and I loved to hang out with the guys. They played dominoes and cards, cursed and drank. For me, this made for some fast excitement in what was otherwise a very dreary and boring atmosphere. I hung out with kids my own age, too. We played double Dutch jump rope and jacks. Vera, who was two years my junior, usually stayed close by except when I wandered up to the liquor store. She was such a Goody Two-shoes she would always turn back.

Grandma did not approve of me hanging out at the liquor store. If it had been up to her, I'd have spent the entire summer sitting on her front porch in an old rocking chair, stringing beans and canning vegetables. All the houses in my grandmother's neighborhood were close together and all the old ladies would sit outside and gossip about their neighbors. They sat there, tearing ends off green beans and husking corn. When I'd pass by, I could overhear them talking about me and my mother. "Mmmm, there goes Essie's girl. Watch out for her 'cause she's going to end up like one of them," they'd always say. One of "them" referred to bad girls who wound up pregnant and no good. Well, they got the pregnant part right, and I was no good for a very long time. But even then I was determined to make something of myself. "You watch, I'm going to be bigger than those stars on TV," I used to tell my grandma. "I'm not living like this. You wait, 'cause I'm going to have a mansion."

Grandma is a moral person who tolerated my selfish attitude. Her self-worth wasn't tied to the value of her house, or
her work as a full-time domestic. What counted to her were
character traits like honesty, integrity, and independence, and
following the teachings of the Bible. What mattered to her
was that she didn't owe anyone and nobody owed her—and
that included the government. She respected people who
worked hard, whether or not they made a lot of money.

If you were poor, she felt you should be content. She never
believed she was impoverished because she always had her
health. That made her feel rich. She never preached this to
me—she said it by setting an example. Everything important
to her was prefaced by the words, "The good Lord said . . ."
In the Bible it says, "Owe no man but to love him," and she
was living testimony to that. Now I understand why poor
people who aren't counting on a government check are some
of the happiest people I know.

As a child, I couldn't understand how people could be
destitute and satisfied, but Grandma was one of those people.
Looking back, I may have been better off than her financially
when I was living on the county, but I was the one who lapsed
into moral decay while relying on a government welfare
check. Grandma kept her moral high ground. She was adamant about not taking government handouts and remaining
self-sufficient. I believe it broke her heart when I went on
welfare.

Growing up, no one in my family ever mentioned welfare.
It was taboo. Even after grandma's husband left her, she
didn't go on welfare. She just grew her fruit and vegetables
and raised her chickens for sale. Along with the little bit of
money she made cleaning houses, that's how she lived.

Years later, after I had married and had my second daughter, I went back to Greenville and paid Grandma Warreno a
visit. I sat on her front porch and understood why she
resented anyone who pitied her because she lived in poverty.

Her attitude was, "I don't feel poor, and I don't need some stranger feeling sorry for me because I don't live in a big house and drive a nice car." She loved her home and her children. That was enough for her.

My grandmother lives a simple life. She's peacefully content with the knowledge that she doesn't have the cares of the world to burden her. She is a good old-fashioned Christian woman who loves God and her independence—and the best role model I ever had.

6
A LITTLE BLACK RACIST

I spent my adolescence blaming most of my troubles on white people. I took it out on my classmates, my teachers, and even strangers. Twice—once in 1969 and once in 1974—I blew up cars belonging to my school teachers.

I can pinpoint the first time I was affected by race. It was 1968 and I was a few months shy of my twelfth birthday. Our family had just moved from the comfort and security of a military base in Japan where my father had been stationed for three years. He was now a technical sergeant working as a flight steward at Scott Air Force Base in Belleville, Illinois.

We were living in one of the worst ghettos in the country, East St. Louis, Illinois. I hated leaving Japan, and when we moved back to America I learned for the first time that every city in the country was on fire. That made me rebel tremendously.

East St. Louis was a dump, an absolute ghetto, totally black and totally separate from the white neighborhoods. The teachers were on strike and the schools were patrolled by armed guards. The playground at Morrison Elementary

School was covered with glass, which we used to pick up with the tips of our fingers and fling at the teachers. They were all white and the kids were all black and we hated each others' guts as much as I hated America.

I tell my friends from South Central Los Angeles all the time: "You all live in paradise. You want to see a ghetto? Go back to East St. Louis." The nice part of town was a city in another state, St. Louis, Missouri. That's where everyone worked, and East St. Louis was the hellish suburb where black folks lived.

I had spent my childhood at schools where I was the only black, and now all my classmates were black. One day I was driving down the street with my mother and I said to her, "I didn't know there were this many black kids in the world."

We lived at 6059 Dickman Place in an off-white three-bedroom ranch house, two blocks off State Street, the main drag. The house we rented was in a little cul-de-sac on the edge of the bad part of town, and behind us there were huge fields, kind of like Huck Finn territory, which separated the neighborhood from a stretch of railroad tracks. I found out later the fields were filled with rows of marijuana plants growing amid the brush and weeds. The police came by one day and torched the fields, forcing my mother to close all the windows to keep us from getting intoxicated.

In our neighborhood, everything shut down at five P.M. And when you went out at night all the stores were closed and barricaded with steel gates. Parts of the neighborhood were burned out by the rioting that took place after the assassination of Dr. Martin Luther King, Jr. National Guardsmen, wearing helmets and wielding rifles and clubs, still patrolled some of our streets.

Not that it helped any. People would walk right into your house and take things. My dad once bought me a bicycle and it was stolen right off our front porch. I couldn't understand why anyone would do that. My parents had tried to protect us all these years by keeping us on military bases, but now we were living in a ghetto and I hated my parents for that. And boy, did I ever let them know it.

In East St. Louis, we'd see my dad sometimes but he wasn't as active in our lives as he was in Japan, when the whole family would go on weekend outings to Tokyo and Mount Fuji. He used to fly around the world and he always brought me back a doll from whatever country he visited, but in East St. Louis, he was around a lot less. After work, he would come home and go to bed. My family was drifting apart and increasingly, I got into even more trouble.

I hung out with older kids and started learning about militant black culture. My parents knew I was up to no good because I stayed out late, vandalizing school buildings and storefronts. They never asked me what I was doing and I guess they didn't really want to know.

That year, I missed a lot of the sixth grade at Morrison Elementary, partly because the teachers were on strike for the first two months of the school calendar. My attitude was, "If the teachers didn't care about showing up, why should I?"

My school only went up to sixth grade, and it was quiet compared to the junior high my sister Avis attended. Clark Junior High was an armed camp where gun-toting guards manned the hallways and teachers kept paddles in their briefcases. I used to go over there because some of the older guys I hung with went to junior high. They were real ghetto gangstas, and these teenage boys appealed to me more than most girls my age. I was a good athlete and had grown into quite a tomboy, so I had no problem keeping up with my new crowd. They treated me like a little sister, a tough one at that, so sex never entered the picture. In my gang, we were preoccupied with getting back at the white man. The older kids told me whites were the ones to blame for poverty and crime.

In East St. Louis, my education came courtesy of my

gangsta friends who would come over to my school looking for trouble and persuade me to join in. When the teachers were picketing, we'd throw bottles at them and challenge them to fights. By the time school started back up for me, I already had a reputation for being one of the bad ones.

The group I hung with liked to go into neighborhoods to loot and burn cars and stores. I wouldn't always participate, but sometimes I'd like to go and watch. I did help make the firebombs. We'd take gas out of a lawn mower and pour it into an empty ten-ounce Coke bottle. Then we'd stuff a rag into the bottle, light it, and throw it at passing cars on State Street or at storefronts.

Once my friends helped me firebomb my teacher's car—solely because she was white. I was really bold. I remember telling my teacher I was going to blow up her car, and I did exactly that. I think she reported me and the school called my parents, but I never heard a word about it. You see, the teachers didn't want to be at school any more than the children. I think they went looking for reasons to get out, so a car bombing certainly certified them for a transfer. And my teacher got one!

As for our school classes, it was all just a waste. We'd throw stuff at our teachers, tear up books, and sit in our chairs with our arms crossed and our feet up on the desks. We'd call the teachers "bitch" and "whitey" and never did any work. The teachers just sat there and called us "darky" and "animals."

In 1970 my dad retired from the Air Force and we moved back to Mount Holly, New Jersey, where we had stayed from 1962 to 1965 when he was stationed at McGuire Air Force Base. In 1970 I turned fourteen and my relationship with my father had changed dramatically. He became a school teacher and we hardly ever talked. He wouldn't even discipline me. I remember him standing in the living room looking out of this big plate glass window. I would be right outside in front of my house with my thumb out trying to hitch a ride, and he would look right through me like I didn't exist. It was as though I lived in a different space and time and my parents weren't there. They were living by that liberal code—"I'm okay, you're okay," so whatever she wants to do is okay by us. My father never made me change my clothes when I wore a skimpy outfit and walked around in a little halter with no bra.

I guess since he felt his mother raised his family on her own, he could leave the responsibility to my mother. He must have assumed that by putting food in the refrigerator and a roof over our heads, he did his job. But it wasn't enough. If parents only knew how much it means to their children for them to be active participants in their lives. My parents weren't there, so I made my own decisions—but I had no moral foundation to base them on. I did what was easy and felt good at the time, and made a bunch of horrible choices. That was the story of my high school years—one terrible decision after another.

We lived in our old house on Woodlane Road. One of the few white people living on my street became a close friend of mine. Her name was Sabra, and even though she was white, my black friends considered her one of us because she was hip, had a black stepdad, and didn't put on airs like some of the other white kids. She was cool and we accepted her. She had long dark hair and was very pretty. Some of the black girls didn't like her because she got the cute black guys, but I still wasn't into boys, so I ended up protecting her.

Besides Sabra, I had a group of friends from the projects. They were fifteen- and sixteen-year-old high school dropouts who were tough and independent, so I looked up to them. There was Frank, Gary, and Anthony, whom we called Big Ant because he was six feet tall and weighed 280 pounds. The only white boy we let hang around with us was a guy named Robert. He came from the local boys' county home where my mother worked as a houseparent. She brought him home one day because he didn't have anywhere to go during the holidays. With his dark, slick-backed hair and a goatee, he looked like a greaser in a James Dean movie. He always wore an oversized sixties-style letterman's sweater draped over his skinny body and a baseball cap on top of his head. He talked with a Jersey accent, and by all appearances seemed like a typical white kid, although he liked hanging around with blacks. We called him "White Rob."

Our idea of a good time was mugging the white military guys who drove through our neighborhood on the way to the base. We called our game "Murphies," a slang expression for tricking someone into doing one thing and then surprising him with something else. The game involved having me dress up like a hooker in a tight skirt, fishnet stockings, high heels, a wig, and a halter top. Then, another neighborhood girl and I would stand in front of a vacant house just three doors down from mine and lure drivers into stopping. Sometimes we were able to coax them into believing we were hookers and that they were going to get some action. Other times I'd run into the street and make up a story about my grandmother collapsing in the house.

Once we got them indoors, the rest of the gang would jump them and grab their money. It was easy disabling our victims with Big Ant, Frank, who weighed about 240 pounds, and the four other guys they had helping them. Usually, we'd incapacitate a guy by slamming the front door into his face as he was entering. Then my friends would knock him down and hold him there while I grabbed his wallet and someone else lifted his watch. Finally, we'd pick the guy up by the arms and tell him to get the hell out and run. Sometimes, if he was really hurt, the gang would help him back to his car. We could do about three Murphies in a day and get a couple hundred dollars. I never saw much of the money. I was just in it for the kicks.

There was another, older guy in his late teens who hung with us named Elijah. He was dark, about two shades darker than me, and wore a full beard. I don't remember him ever holding a job, but his pockets were always full of cash. He talked smooth, moved deliberately, and was very sexy. I had a wild crush on him. One summer day in 1973 after my sophomore year in high school, I found out how he earned a living. We went for a drive to Brown Mills, a white town near Mount Holly. We pulled up to a beautiful house and Elijah asked me to stay outside behind some bushes and watch for people. He broke inside and came out with TVs, stereos, and jewelry. He was careful and watched the clock, never making more than three trips inside a house. We probably did about ten houses that school year and never got caught. He had a little car, a black Dodge Charger, and we'd fill it with what we could get and head back home. Because I was in it for a good time and didn't want my parents to catch on, I let Elijah keep most of the loot. He dropped out of sight later that year and I learned he had gone away to prison. That wasn't the last of Elijah, though. I was destined to meet up with him again two years later, after graduation.

Robbing white guys and burglarizing homes weren't the only diversions I had in the summer of '73. A few months before my seventeenth birthday, my dad helped me get a part-time job answering phones at McGuire Air Force Base. I met an older white guy, a twenty-six-year-old captain named Kevin. He was a tall, good-looking man with dusty blond hair and a nice build. He drove a white Corvette, and when he started to show an interest in me I was swept right off my stylish platform shoes.

He used to drive past my house on his way to the base and wave, and one day he walked up to me while I was working and said, "I've seen you around, what's your name?" The next time I saw him, he gave me and my friend Linda a ride in his Corvette.

Kevin must have assumed that I was fast, probably because of the provocative way I dressed. You know—my Pam Grier look. In the office, I flirted with him all the time. He'd tell me, "You're too young to be going out with me," and I would say, "Nope, I can go out with anybody I want to."

I grew up dreaming of moving to Hollywood someday and I cast this golden man as my Robert Redford. I told him everything about me, including all the trouble I had gotten into, so he probably figured I was wise way beyond my years.

One day at work we made a date. That night, I left the house wearing jeans and a sweatshirt, then ducked into an alley to change into something more sleazy: a miniskirt, halter top, fishnets, and a pair of platform shoes that made me appear six feet tall with my afro. I walked down to the 7-Eleven, which was about a half block from my house, and spotted the captain waiting for me in his 'Vette. I got in his car and he told me I looked real good. I smiled back at him. Then he explained he had to stop by his apartment to pick something up, uh-huh . . .

Kevin was nice to me and up to this point in my life, I hadn't known many cordial white men. I was just this naive black girl working part-time at an Air Force base. Well, the second I walked through the door of his apartment he jumped me, and, well—I went for it! I didn't even have a chance to sit down. We were making out and I realized he wanted a lot more than I was willing to give. I had some boyfriends and had done some petting, but I was still a virgin. I had never asked my parents about sex, or even asked my friends if they had ever tried it. I feared if my black male friends started having sex with me, they wouldn't let me hang with them anymore. So I had kept men at a safe distance up to this point. I told Kevin, "Man, I'm not interested in sex." He said, "Oh come on, I know you've done this before."

I didn't want to have sex and continued to tell him that, but he kept pressuring me. I went along with it, but I was scared. I didn't know if he was going to go crazy on me. After we got our clothes off, he tried to have intercourse with me and he realized, "Oh man, this girl's a virgin. She's not opening up." So he made me get in a bathtub full of hot water, as if that would make it easier for me to have sex.

After I got out of the tub, it wasn't any easier. To this very day, I still think about this moment and I'm not even sure if we ever had intercourse. Eventually he just stopped and said, "I'm taking you home," in an irritated voice.

Initially, I didn't think it was a big deal or that he took advantage of me. But I resented him for exposing an innocent side of me that up until then I had successfully hidden from everyone I knew.

I kept working at the base and I'd run into him all the time. Gradually, it occurred to me that what he did was wrong. He should have stopped after I said "No." He also should never have been seducing teenagers. What he did to me was sickening, and I soon began to hate all white people even more for what had happened. I mean, this was someone whom I respected because my father had always taught us that you salute these people. His highfalutin blue uniform and those silver captain's bars on his shoulders had really impressed me. I was also a sucker.

Looking back on it today, I know that incident with the captain was statutory rape, as I was only sixteen. I never told anyone about it. Instead, I began taking it out on the white kids who went to my school, Rancocas Valley High. I'd corner kids, beat them up, and steal their lunch money. My targets were especially those boys who didn't play football and were just into their school work. Math and science geeks were much easier to beat on than some jock.

I also became promiscuous. I didn't sleep with white guys, just black men, older black men from the military base. I was now committed to hating white people and was never going to trust one again.

All through high school, and even prior to that, my white counselors and teachers expressed what they called compassion and understanding. Instead of identifying a single factor at the root of my anger, the school psychologists said my ancestral past, filled with persecution and discrimination, were at the core of my rebellious behavior. My attitude to that line of garbage was "That's cool," and I went about my business. It was payback time.

My track coach, Mr. Butler, was different from the other white teachers and counselors. I was one of the best runners on the team, running the 220 and the high hurdles. He was also hard on me. He did not like me smoking cigarettes and getting high.

I was frustrated that Mr. Butler never seemed to let up on me, so at the end of my junior year, I decided to quit track. He was the only teacher who asked me about what I was planning to do with my future. He used to tell me I could have a career in track, that if I practiced and studied hard, I might be able to earn a college scholarship. He even hinted I had the potential to try out for the Olympics. To tell you the truth, my interests were in partying and Mr. Butler was getting on my nerves.

After I quit the team, he got very angry and said that I was making a big mistake. So one day, he and his wife showed up at my house to talk to my parents. He told them I was ruining my life. The nerve of that white man! So the next day after school, I went up to his car, stuffed a bunch of gasoline-soaked rags deep into the gas tank, and set it on fire. I turned away and began to sprint, much faster than Mr. Butler ever would have seen me run because my adrenaline was pumping and I was afraid somebody might spot me. As I turned the corner to get off campus, I smelled the burning fuel and then heard the car ignite with a big whoosh. When I looked over my shoulder, I saw the car engulfed in orange, yellow, and red flames. Then there was a small explosion, more like a sudden poof. As I kept running, I could hear the sounds of broken pieces of metal and shards of glass hitting the pavement. Like an assassin who prefers to kill from a distance because he can't stomach his work, I did the deed and never peeked back for another look. Somehow, that made it a little easier for me to live with myself.

Mr. Butler never found out it was me who torched his car, but I suspect he had a good idea. I rarely felt bad when I did stuff, but that night as I lay in my bed staring at the ceiling, I felt remorse. In my heart I knew this man was trying to help me get out of my gutter. I just couldn't cope with a white person who was actually taking an interest in me. I assumed they were all racists and not to be trusted, particularly the white teachers and other adult authority figures in my life. For the first time, I began looking deep within my soul and saw what had previously been invisible to me: I wasn't merely reacting to discrimination or bigotry, but had become a racist myself, and that was the cold reality of it all. For years, I used racism as an excuse to break the law and justify my rude and immature behavior. I was angry with the world and shouldn't have been. Truth be known, there had been many Mr. Butlers in my life who believed in me—both white and black— including my parents, aunts, uncles, cousins, and several teachers, all of whom knew I had potential and tried to tell me exactly that. I was just too stubborn and selfish to recognize any good in me, or in people like Mr. Butler. It would take me several more years and dozens of more missteps before I would learn to trust someone of a different color than my own.

7

SOME KINDA'
GRADUATE

As I began my senior year, I didn't think about going away to college. I was far too much of a rebel for that. I continued spending most of my time running the streets and partying at the base with my close friends from school, Karen and Linda. College just never came up. My high school counselor never talked to me about it. For that matter, he never talked to me about much at all. I had requested him because he was black and my previous counselor, a white woman, never brought up the possibility of college. She informed me blacks were better off working with their hands. Her advice was that I get a job after graduation and not go to school. Well, as far as I was concerned, whites ran the businesses and I wasn't about to work for a honky! I think my black counselor resented me for switching to him because he wanted to appear neutral. He wasn't into black issues and when I complained about whites, he used to tell me, "Now, Larstella, don't bring that here."

I did a pretty good job of keeping my street life a secret from my parents until I finally got arrested for shoplifting. It happened in the summer before my senior year. My girlfriend

Karen and I were planning on borrowing my mother's car for the weekend to take a trip to the shore in Atlantic City. I needed a bathing suit so we decided to go pick one up at a strip mall in the town of Burlington, about a twenty-minute drive from my house.

I was now working as a waitress at a truck stop on the interstate and could have bought the bathing suit, but that wasn't the point. I stole things all the time and had never been charged before. Since I was a minor, I got off with warnings. This time I went into the department store and put on the suit under my clothes in the changing room. The security guards grabbed me just as I was walking out the door, and they weren't fooling around this time. They called the police and had me arrested. They searched Karen, found nothing on her, and let her go. The police took me to the station and booked me. They didn't cuff me, but I got to ride in the back seat of their cruiser, and bad as I was, I actually thought it was cool. I couldn't wait to tell Big Ant. I knew he'd be impressed. It wasn't every day you got arrested and taken for a ride to the "big house." Of course, I didn't have a clue that a shoplifting conviction on my record could stay with me for the rest of my life.

At the station, I gave my real name. I wasn't embarrassed at all, so when they took my picture I smiled broadly for the camera just in case it ended up in the newspaper the next day. The police photographer didn't like that and took another shot. I also got fingerprinted and searched. The police weren't mean, they were very matter-of-fact. This was routine to them. Then I got some harsh news: they were going to put me in jail until I could make bail. Well damn, suddenly, the glamour of doing time in the big house was gone. I told them, "You can't do that—I'm only seventeen." But since I had no identification or any proof of my age, they put me behind bars. I was nervous and scared, so I put on my tough girl act and pretended it didn't bother me in the least. I mean, I could certainly play "bad."

Later, I called home, and got a message from my sister Vera that my mother had decided I should stay in jail overnight in order to learn a lesson. So I spent my first night in jail hanging out with a bunch of real live hookers, not little amateur punks like me.

My father picked me up the next day and he was in a state of shock. He told me I was the first Irby ever to have been arrested. He asked, "And how do you feel about that, Larstella?" My mom gave me a good tongue lashing but thankfully I didn't get my butt whipped. I was a little too big for that. The next day, one of my girlfriends told me, "You won't get a job now 'cause you have a record." I wasn't worried. I told her I'd make my own job.

Looking back, I was quite a fool. I would have been better off if both the system and my parents had been more punitive. Our judicial system must be a place where a first-time offender will say, "I don't want to come back through here again." What I really needed was some tough love.

Troubled youth would be better served if the courts, schools, and families worked in unison to monitor a delinquent teen's behavior. I didn't get the message that there were consequences to my actions, so not long after my family paid the $300 fine, I was back at that same mall stealing again and again.

Delinquent kids need to feel some shame, fear, and embarrassment. We are so quick now to blame an individual's behavior on larger societal issues—such as racism and poverty—that our traditional deterrents to crime are meaningless.

As the time passed, my family pretended my arrest had never happened. Late in my senior year, my friends were moving on. Robert went to another home for boys. I heard Big

Ant and Frank had gotten arrested and sent to jail, but I never did find out what for. I had no plans after graduation in June 1975, but I knew it was time to leave home. Not that I had a serious choice. My mother's house rule was that after you earned your diploma, you had to leave home. I was eighteen when I packed up my brother's car—he was in Germany serving in the Air Force—and moved to Philadelphia. I got a job working in a black-owned record store in nearby Camden, New Jersey. It was there that I decided I was going to save some money and move to Hollywood, California. I wasn't sure what I was going to do there except for one thing—dance alongside Don Cornelius on *Soul Train* and experience the glamorous life. I couldn't boogie well, but I sure looked the part.

The record store job was fab. I sat behind the counter and listened to Isaac Hayes and Sly and the Family Stone all day long. The owners were never there and I liked my autonomy. I spent a lot of time next door at a restaurant owned by a group of Muslims. They talked all day about Malcolm X and Elijah Muhammad and how all blacks would unite for the revolution that would result in the formation of a separate state for the American black race. I hadn't heard radical talk like that since I was a kid in East St. Louis.

What impressed me most about the Muslims was their respectful manners and their conservative lifestyle. They dressed impeccably, kept their bodies clean, and refused to eat pork. The men were ambitious and entrepreneurial. They loathed crime and felt blacks should contribute more to society. At the time, I agreed with their views on white racism and black independence. They also demanded that their women not drink, smoke, or dress suggestively. That was the one thing I didn't get. I would have made a lousy Muslim because I loved my clothes and had no intention of giving them up.

One day at work, an Italian customer walked in the record

shop and started flirting with me. He became a regular customer and after a while started calling me "Star" because *Stella*, part of my name, means "star" in Italian. So that became my nickname, which was perfect for someone dreaming of living in Hollywood someday.

The Italian guy was the first person I ever let call me something other than Larstella. Pretty soon, my bosses were calling me Star and my girlfriends picked up on it, too. That summer when I needed to have my front tooth capped because of a crack I had received in a fight years earlier, I had the dentist design a silver cap with the middle cut out in the shape of a star. And after that, everyone called me Star.

Living in Philadelphia was exciting. I was meeting a lot of guys and hitting the dance clubs. One night I bumped into an old pal from Mount Holly who had been a bad influence on me—Elijah, the guy I used to fantasize about and also burglarize houses with. After talking with him for ten minutes, my old attraction for him resurfaced like the goose bumps I got when he first spoke to me.

I told him I loved working at the Camden record shop but hated where I was living. He said his sister had a spare room for rent and she would probably let me live with her. But there was a catch—he needed me for a job: robbing a liquor store. The outlaw in him made my body quiver with excitement, so I agreed to go along and be Bonnie to his sly Clyde.

A week after talking to him, I moved into his sister's house. The next day, he picked me up in his same old Charger and we drove to a small town outside Trenton, New Jersey. I dressed the role of an urban bandit—khakis, a T-shirt, and a green Army jacket. We parked around a corner, about a hundred feet from the store. When we walked through the door, there was a little Chinese man behind the counter. Elijah pulled out his gun and told the man to fill the paper bag I was holding with money. After the clerk emptied the register, I stuck $400 into my jacket and ran out of the store behind Elijah. It happened so fast, I don't even remember feeling scared until I was back at the car.

When I turned to look at Elijah, the expression on his face alarmed me. He was petrified, and I had never seen him like that before. The man who had taught Frank, Big Ant, and all my old friends how to do all this bad stuff and get away with it suddenly looked extremely vulnerable. I started feeling very nervous. I was sweating, gasping for air, and thinking, "Oh my God, somebody could have shot us." I even realized that Elijah could have gunned down the Chinese man and as Elijah's accomplice, I could be living permanently in the big house.

As I sat in Elijah's car, I started to think seriously about what the hell I was doing robbing a liquor store in the first place. I thought back to the time I lit up Mr. Butler's car and I had that same sickening feeling in the pit of my stomach.

When I got back home, Elijah's sister knew I had done a job with her brother, and she was fuming. She had two daughters and warned me that she did not want that kind of activity going on under her roof. "Girl," she said, "you're into a lawless life and you're not going to do this stuff around my daughters!" She probably would have booted me out right then if she hadn't needed the rent money so badly. I promised her there would be no more trouble with me, and I didn't see Elijah after that. Then I heard from his sister he had been arrested again. She took it out on me and the situation in the house became unbearable. In December, she told me to leave and I packed my bags and left. I was anxious to move on but had no place to go, so I moved into the record store.

The Muslims next door encouraged me to set a goal, and I decided to focus on my goal of saving money for the California move. However, this time there would be no more stealing and robbing. I called my mother and asked if I could come home. She said okay since I had my job at the record store and

I told her I would be moving out west on April 1 — no fooling. I even took on a second job on an assembly line at a plant that manufactured nuts and bolts. My shift was from midnight to six A.M. and my job was to inspect the hardware as it came off the conveyor belt and take the flawed bolts from the line. My feet always ached and my nails got filthy, but I managed to save every penny from that job for my big trip to California.

In a high school yearbook belonging to a dear friend, I wrote the following passage: "To my Super Special Best Friend. One day when our dreams come true, we will both sit back in our million-dollar houses and laugh. While we continue to swing in Mount Hollywood, maybe we'll make it in the real Hollywood."

My friend changed her mind at the last minute. She stayed behind in New Jersey while Karen, the girl I was with when I got nabbed for shoplifting, made the trip across country with me. All winter long, I kept thinking, "California, here we come." On April Fool's Day, I left Mount Holly with $300 in my pocket and ten boxes of clothes and record albums. Karen and I had an eight-track tape player with us and listened to Funkadelic for the entire ride out. Now Hollywood, that's where it was *happening!*

8

THE STARSHIP ENTERPRISE™

Seven years after arriving in Los Angeles, I decided it was time to earn an honest living. I was going to stop scheming, but the problem with going off welfare cold turkey was that it left me broke. By September 1983 I had no job prospects, rent was due, Angel was hungry, and I was praying, "If I'm not supposed to be living on the county, I do need a miracle."

My alma mater, Woodbury University, kept a jobs listing board, so I called to see if they had any postings. A company called Rycoff, a condiments distributor, was advertising for a customer service representative. The job required two days a week and paid $10 an hour. I called and got the supervisor on the phone. When I asked about the position, there was a dead silence.

Then he said, "I put that ad up two weeks ago, one at Woodbury and one at the University of Southern California. I got twelve calls from USC and you're the first call from Woodbury." He said he had two openings and wanted to fill them with a graduate from each school. I knew right then that the job was mine.

It was a great feeling, but I still had to fill out an application. After I received the paperwork in the mail, I figured I would type it up to impress the supervisor. Then I got this idea to write it out by hand. Sure enough, the job required good penmanship since you had to fill out orders legibly. The day after I sent back the application, I was asked to come in for an interview.

The man in charge was a small elderly white guy. For years, I hadn't trusted white people. There was that captain who date-raped me, and all those teachers who never showed any faith in my abilities. There were national black voices always reminding us that whites had enslaved us, humiliated us, and were our enemy.

But in the past year, since I had started going to church, my attitude toward white people had substantially changed. Pastor Price stressed that all Christian people were our brothers and sisters—black and white. Having a child had mellowed me significantly and finishing college had also helped to change my outlook. Many of my professors were white, and unlike the teachers and guidance counselors I encountered growing up, they took my ideas and opinions very seriously. The respect they showed me was gratefully returned.

Truth be told, I only began trusting whites because Pastor Price said it was the right thing to do. He preached against racism and reverse racism. From his pulpit, he would say that white people weren't the enemy—the devil was the enemy. And somehow—from that day on, I didn't hate white people anymore. I decided they deserved the benefit of the doubt.

The manager at Rycoff was nice in a distant way and I was very respectful toward him. So I told him about my work experience and the classes I had taken at Woodbury. He said he'd get back to me and by the time I got home, he had called and left a message that I could start working right away. It was terrific news seeing as my rent check was due the following week.

In order to work, I put Angel in day care, which I paid for on a sliding scale. My job at Rycoff was to take calls from field salesmen and process their orders for mustard, ketchup, and relish. It was a far cry from dancing on *Soul Train*, but at least it was money. By January 1984, I had increased my hours and I was making $400 in a good week.

Then I started getting pressure to join the workers' union. A black woman named Sarah was really on my case. She had been working at the same job, at the same company, for fifteen years. Man, I couldn't even fathom that kind of life. She wanted me to join the union, so I asked her, "What's in it for me?"

As you can imagine, Sarah and I didn't click. We were the only blacks in the office so we would pretend to be friendly, but when people were out of earshot, she hassled me about the guild. "Oh, let me explain to you some more about our union." They were telling people we needed to go out on strike, and I was like, "You kiddin', right?"

The main reason I wasn't joining was because the union wanted $230 up front in dues. I said: "Tell me exactly what I get for two hundred thirty dollars?" (I'm a shopper—I don't buy anything unless I get something in return.) And joining this union was not the first thing on my mind. Now that I was off welfare, and that safety cushion had been removed, my mind had transformed into the *Starship Enterprise*—going places where I had only dreamed of before. With no intention of staying in the condiments business for too long, I was thinking of starting my own business. When I finally told the union organizers no, my co-workers got very angry. They stopped talking to me at the water cooler and even ignored me when they passed by my desk.

Sorry, Mr. Upton Sinclair, but I've subsequently grown to have a real distaste for unions. They may have been necessary once to improve working conditions, but I also know they were created in the industrial North to keep migrating black laborers from the South out of the work force. During the Jim Crow era, blacks were moving North for jobs because of the harsh treatment they were receiving below the Mason-Dixon line. They were willing to work for lower wages and this angered many of the northern white blue-collar workers.

Sarah belonged to the union and in my opinion she was a slow worker. We were supposed to take orders quickly so the salesmen could get on to the next location. Yet Sarah appeared to take as few calls as she could and her conversations dragged on forever. She gossiped all day with the salesmen on the phone, and I thought to myself, "Why should she have any say over how much money she made?" She used to claim I was being ripped off because I didn't have any benefits. Then again, to me $10 an hour was pretty good money. I felt sorry for her because she had been at Rycoff for years and had not been promoted at all. How could she not want to advance?

Shortly after I told the union to forget it, they called for a strike and demanded I join the picket line. Again, I told them no. When I came to work the next morning, the membership was having a meeting outside the office. When I got close to where they were huddling, they started yelling at me and warned me that they were not going to let me cross. I turned around, went home, and never went back.

Part of their eventual settlement included a provision that management fire the part-timers and agree to a closed shop, which required all employees to belong to the union. I was out and it would be a long time coming before I ever worked for someone other than myself again.

"You're getting away from your vision." That's what my friend Kenneth, who ran the ad agency where I worked the summer before Angel was born, kept telling me the whole time I was working at Rycoff. Before leaving the company, I had an idea to start my own magazine. At church I was making new friends, and one day we were talking about the plight of the single black Christian. I heard all these don'ts about drinking, smoking, and having sex, but what and where were the do's? What could we do to have fun? Where could a nice Christian woman like myself meet a nice Christian guy?

I was single and wanted to socialize—anything to get out of watching TV on a Friday night. I knew people at other churches and they would tell us things that were going on: ski trips, roller skating outings, parties, and dances, but it was all done by word of mouth. One of my male friends said we needed an events calendar for single young Christians, and I thought it was a brilliant idea.

Now I was ready to go for it. Since my friends weren't interested in helping me with the start-up, I began pounding the pavement on my own. The idea was simply to gather all the information on social functions at various churches in South Central, compile them in a magazine, and then distribute it to churches around town for free.

I wanted this magazine to appeal to different denominations so I started flipping through the Bible for a name. I came across Hebrews 10:25, a passage about people coming together to do good works. There was a line, "Not forsaking the assembling of ourselves together, as the manner of some, but exhorting one another . . ." That's it, I thought to myself. I called it *Not Forsaking the Assembling—N.F.T.A.* for short.

My friends in advertising told me about a program run by the Small Business Administration called SCORE. I went to their downtown Los Angeles office and met some retirees who told me how to apply for a business license and write up a small business plan. I discovered other leads as well. One day I was in the Bank of America to close my dismal savings account and found a booklet on writing business plans just lying on a counter. Then, I went to the library and took out some how-to books on business start-ups.

Over the years, I've heard liberals whine that the poor and

minorities don't have access to information. I don't buy it. Anyone can walk into a public library, and if someone doesn't let you in, I suggest you get on the horn with Miss Rosa Parks. The information I got was all free, and I learned the only obstacle holding me back was myself.

I decided to pick out ten of the largest black churches in Los Angeles to approach about publishing their monthly social calendars. They'd give me the information over the phone and I'd write it down. Pretty soon they loved to hear my voice because I listed their events for free. The churches were all black and of different denominations: Charismatic, Baptist, Apostolic, and Church of God in Christ. Increasingly, the single men and women of these churches wanted to meet new people.

Since I did not have any money for office equipment, I looked to my friends to cut corners. I had an acquaintance in my apartment building named Jeff who sold Panasonic memory typewriters. After work, he let me borrow the demo model he showed clients. With that, I typed up my notes and produced the calendar.

Then I just went knocking on doors. That part came easy for me. I was an extrovert and loved meeting new people. In the old days, those skills came in handy when I wanted to meet new guys or connect with friends who were tied into the party scene. Now I was meeting a different group of people— individual entrepreneurs. While these men and women weren't sophisticated or well-heeled, I admired them because they had mustered the energy to start their own businesses. They were mechanics, bakers, gas station owners, hair dressers, and real estate brokers, folks from all walks of life who were proud of their independence and were willing to take a risk to strike out on their own. Now, I was one of them, and proud of it.

The first minister I called on was Bishop Charles Blake of

the West Angeles Church of God in Christ. To look the part of an ad salesman, I borrowed a beautiful burgundy portfolio briefcase from one of my new roommates, Yvonne. Leona loaned me a business suit but told me I had to have it dry cleaned right away because she needed to wear it later in the week. I couldn't drive my moped long distances without ruining my dress and hair, so another friend drove me to the appointment. On most calls I took the bus, and I was careful to get off one stop before the destination so nobody would think a publisher was taking the bus to make business appointments. While that might be okay in New York, in Los Angeles you need a set of wheels and a hip pair of shades!

Every Sunday, Bishop Blake sermonized a congregation of nine thousand during three services. I went into his office, sat down, and made my presentation. After I was finished, he said, "You really are going to do this, aren't you?" I said yes, and he called in his accountant and told him to draw me up a check for $100. My first check! For the next eight years, Bishop Blake bought an ad in every magazine I printed. For my first issue, I sold sixteen ads just like that.

My first white advertiser was a grocery store called the 32nd Street Market. It was located near the University of Southern California, and I'll never forget the day I made that sale because I got the biggest check I had ever seen in my life. Keep in mind my other advertisers paid $100 to $200 an issue. My full-page rate was $250, which was too low, I found out later. The owner, Leo, was so impressed with the magazine he wrote me a $2,000 check on the spot and advertised with me for one full year.

MOVING ON UP

One of the biggest impediments to striking out on my own was my living situation. As I got closer to the publication of my first issue, I started feeling a bad vibe from my envious roommates. Since quitting the county, the atmosphere in the apartment had become very tense and I was beginning to think it was time to move on. We had only one phone and it was constantly ringing for me. When one of the kids answered, I would grab it away just in case it was one of my clients.

Still, I managed to sell $2,000 in advertising my first month (this didn't include the check from the 32nd Street Market, because they didn't become a client until later). Because my printer was a friend who agreed to carry a balance on what I owed, I used part of the money to move into my own apartment. I found a one-bedroom back on Ardmore for $360 a month.

Then I suffered a terrible setback. After I got into a fight with my printer, I abruptly went elsewhere. Changing printers was the biggest mistake I ever made. My new printer charged me $10,000 for each run. I didn't find out he was billing me that much until I was $20,000 in debt. He originally promised to charge me at my previous rate, but when I asked for the bill, he said, "Don't worry about it." I should have.

I begged my old printer to take me back and fortunately he agreed. But eventually my debt climbed to $30,000 with interest and late charges, and years later I wound up in bankruptcy court over this liability. It was one long, hard, and expensive learning experience.

Despite this crisis, I forged ahead. From June 1984 to June 1985, I published ten issues, distributed 100,000 magazines, and deposited $50,000 in the bank. In my second issue, I doubled the number of ads. That fall, when I landed the 32nd Street Market ad, I bought a used white Peugeot for $800 and acted like it was a new Mercedes. Money was tight because of my printing costs, but an advertiser friend loaned me $10,000 to keep going. Angel and I had our best Christmas ever!

Of course personally, I wasn't getting rich. I had to pay rent, as well as printing costs and commissions to two sales people I had hired. After I prepared their sales kits, they went out and sold ads. My old roommate Penny came in every day to help answer phones and do some light typing and filing. I paid her a couple hundred dollars a month under the table because she was still on AFDC welfare and that's all I could afford.

Was I taking advantage of her? I didn't think so. Penny got me thinking about how wrong the welfare system was. Penny had to live a lie. She was coming to my apartment every day at eight-thirty A.M., sometimes with her daughter, and staying there all day to work. I couldn't pay her enough to get her off the county, but she didn't mind because she was learning skills she wouldn't be able to pick up anywhere else. Over time, I increased her pay, but I surely couldn't give her minimum wage and cover the taxes for Workers' Compensation, disability, and Social Security. That would have made me broke. Yet I don't know what I would have done without her. She was integral to my start-up, and also kept an eye on Angel when I went out on calls.

The way the welfare system is set up, she couldn't report that couple hundred dollars a month on her CA-7 form or they'd deduct it from her welfare check. People on welfare should be allowed to work in entry-level jobs in small neighborhood businesses. And as long as they're developing skills, I feel they should be able to keep the welfare money and the minimum-wage income. Just keep a time limit on the benefits. That way people can get back on their feet without exploiting the system for an indefinite period of time. A couple of years later, I gave Penny a raise to $200 a week and she was able to quit welfare. Before long, she found a higher-paying job working as a clerk for an insurance company.

CONSPIRING AGAINST ENTREPRENEURS

I have a major gripe against government: they don't make it easy to stay in business. When I was starting up my magazine, dealing with the government bureaucracy was much harder than collecting AFDC welfare, food stamps, WIC stickers, and a Medi-Cal card. I can relate to a bumper sticker I once saw on the freeway driving to work: "Make getting welfare as hard as getting a building permit."

The regulations I ran up against seemed designed to discourage entrepreneurship. Immediately after I filed a fictitious name statement with the Los Angeles County Clerk's office, I began receiving those dreaded envelopes labeled "Official Government Document." Before long, I felt like a little black mouse trying to maneuver through an endless bureaucratic maze.

The first inquiry was from the Employment Development Department (EDD) in Sacramento. They wanted to know if I had any employees they could tax. I thought of telling them about Penny, but I decided I couldn't afford to be honest without putting the business in jeopardy.

The next agency I heard from was the city of Los Angeles. They called and asked to inspect my place of business. Their interest was making sure that running my magazine didn't conflict with any zoning requirements or violate any environmental regulations. I'd explained to them over the phone that

I didn't own any printing equipment and only sold ads from my home, but that wasn't sufficient. They insisted on seeing it for themselves so I had to cancel some appointments and host a city inspector for a tour of my one-bedroom apartment.

In time, I also heard from the IRS, the state tax board, and county tax collector's office, all wanting information on my revenues. Annual accountability wasn't sufficient. They wanted quarterly income projections and quarterly prepaid tax payments based on that revenue.

I couldn't comprehend any of this paperwork, nor did I have the time to research it. I was too busy trying to build my advertising base so I could pay my printing bills every month. Should I have hired someone to deal with the red tape? I would have loved to but I could barely afford to pay myself a salary, let alone hire an accountant. I felt like telling all these agencies to leave me alone and come back later after my business had made a little money.

I struggled in those early months, taking home $600 to $700 a month. While I wasn't doing much better financially than I did in my welfare days, I sure felt better about myself.

Living on a tight budget and working so hard, I lost a lot of weight. My friends wondered if I was getting enough to eat. I wasn't, but I think I was so satisfied being on my own that it got me through those days when the rent was due and I had to go hungry so my daughter Angel could eat.

One experience in particular made it all worthwhile. I had been off welfare about two years and decided to open a checking account with one of my customers, Family Savings Bank. I deposited $4,000—one month's advertising revenue. As I left the bank, it hit me that it was not a whole lot less than what I took in for the year on AFDC welfare. I knew right then I would never go back to living on the county. I could now earn an income on my own without some government watchdog asking me to fill out a form every month explaining whom I was living with, what was in my fridge, and what I was putting in my bank account. I had finally realized that living on the county had come at the expense of my autonomy and my self-esteem. A welfare check is no substitute for the pride and self-satisfaction that comes from reaping the rewards of your labor, even with Big Brother government still watching your every move.

9

ROSEY GRIER FINDS ME A HUSBAND

A church friend of mine named Diane moved into my apartment building in 1984 and we quickly became even closer friends. She was a secretary working for Hall of Fame football player Rosey Grier, who was now heading up a Christian youth outreach program called Are You Committed. Her office was located in downtown Los Angeles, where Rosey ran the center from an old warehouse that included a gymnasium and a retail clothing store that raised money for his program through the sale of athletic gear donated from large manufacturers.

On Saturdays, Rosey's employees and volunteers would fan out into skid row to urge all the alcoholics, drug addicts, and homeless people to give up their lifestyles. They'd also talk about God and direct these people to places where they could get help. The term for this type of intervention is *street witnessing*. You could also find Rosey's missionaries on the streets of South Central Los Angeles, including Jordan Downs, one of the city's toughest housing projects. Over hot dog and hamburger barbecues, they'd tell folks how the Lord offered a better way and Rosey would invite the children to the AYC center to play sports and do arts and crafts with him. (Rosey, as you might have read somewhere, is a wonderful needlepointer.)

Diane kept bugging me to do a write-up on AYC for my magazine, and I kept putting her off because I was too busy selling ad space. Then one Saturday in November, I found some free time to pay a visit. That day, AYC was organizing a trip to Orange County to watch a broadcast of the national religious TV show hosted by televangelists Paul and Jan Crouch. The guy in charge of the outing was a white man named Peter Pentecost Parker. I brought along Angel, who had just turned four and was full of energy. She took an immediate liking to Peter on the hour-long bus trip to the Trinity Broadcasting Network in Anaheim. I was a little surprised because Angel had never met a white man before.

Peter was forty-three then, fifteen years older than me. He worked as a missionary in Rosey's program and was very nice, but I was baffled by him. I thought to myself, "What is this white dude doing working with all these black folks?"

So on the bus ride back, I talked to him for a little while. He was assisting a pastor at a charismatic church in Thousand Oaks and had volunteered to work with Rosey five months earlier after seeing him on a television show. He asked me about my magazine business and he told me he earned his living as a door-to-door salesman. That night, when I was getting Angel ready for bed, she told me she wished Peter was her daddy. She always brought this up after she had spent some time bonding with a male friend of mine. She had met Jerry, her father, only once, so I promised her I'd keep an eye open for one.

Peter called me the next day, and the day after that. He gave me plenty of sales tips so most of our early conversations centered around my magazine. His favorite line was "God has a dollar out there for me, but I might have to open ten doors to get a dime from each to collect that dollar."

Then he invited me to his house in Thousand Oaks for Thanksgiving. He lived in a room in a home and the owners, who were out of town, had allowed him to host a party for the holiday. I went with Angel and Diane and we were joined by some of her co-workers from AYC. They even brought along a couple of homeless people.

We cooked a turkey and brought in some pies and hot vegetables. Peter picked up right where he left off with Angel, playing and talking with her. Until that day, I thought of him mostly as a friend, but by the time we left that night, I felt a spark of attraction toward him.

At church the following Sunday, Diane noticed Peter in the congregation. I whispered to her, "Is Peter seeing anyone?"

She said she didn't think so, and then I asked her, "Why don't you date him?"

She answered, "No, I'm not into white boys."

I replied, "Well, I think he's kinda cute."

Later that week, I invited him over for dinner. My apartment was decorated with wicker furniture and a pair of large multicolored oriental fans hanging from the living room ceiling. I served him a traditional down-home meal—ox tails, collard greens, black-eyed peas, and candied yams. It was Peter's first taste of southern cooking, and I had to explain what each dish was. "White people in the South eat this too," I said, needling him a little. We had gotten to know each other very well in a very short period of time. After I put Angel to bed, we sat down in my living room for a cup of coffee. That's when he told me he could see us spending the rest of our lives together.

He officially proposed two months later, and our relationship changed significantly. He started visiting every night on his way home from work. When Angel was asleep, we'd sit together and hold hands. His drive home took an hour, and when it would get to be eleven P.M., I usually invited him to sleep on the couch. He always said, "No, absolutely not," even though he had to be at work by seven the next morning. He wanted to avoid any hint of impropriety.

Still, it was all happening so fast I didn't feel as though I could give him an answer right away. I had always said to my friends that I wasn't going to get married for a long time. But I also had Angel to consider. She needed a father, and Peter certainly appeared to fill that job description. I also was feeling some pressure from other quarters. Now that I was running my magazine, I was meeting numerous men and getting a lot of dinner invitations. Jerry had finished school and returned from San Francisco. He wanted to visit Angel and I began wondering for her sake whether I should be married to him. Still, Jerry was not religious at all, and in this respect, I believed Peter and I were much more compatible.

The one thing Peter and I tried not to let interfere with our plans was the color of our skin. We figured most of our Christian friends weren't going to criticize our relationship. My reluctance revolved around more commonplace issues, like our fifteen-year age difference and how we would make ends meet. In Ecclesiastes, it says, "Two are better than one," so we figured we could get by on what I made from the magazine and Peter's modest salary working for Rosey. In January, we paid Rosey a visit and set a wedding date for March 2, 1985.

I'm not sure Peter realized what he was letting himself in for by getting involved with me. Since I started going to church and listening to Pastor Price's sermons on racial harmony, I had been able to look at white people in a new light, but my exposure to them was limited. It was the same for Peter in regard to blacks. He grew up in Pompton Plains, a white community in northern New Jersey. That town was a tiny place, with one set of streetlights and a police chief everybody knew.

By my standards, Peter came from money. He was raised in a three-bedroom, two-story house that sat on three acres. His father was Robert Burns Parker, a vice president for a company called Pennsylvania Refining Company, which was eventually bought out by Pennzoil. Peter was the second of four kids and his mom was a housewife. Her name was Wyntje Pentecost, she was Dutch, and her father was the famous Christian composer George Frederick Pentecost. She also came from money—when she graduated from boarding school, her parents bought her a Stutz Bearcat automobile.

Peter attended Rutgers University in the 1960s, but he didn't want to go into the oil business like his father. He was a rebel like me and got into drugs. Eventually he became a heroin addict, which led to the breakup of his first marriage. Then one night in 1978 he took a bottle of Valium, lined up each 10-milligram tablet on a table, and took them with a pint of rum. Lucky for him his ex-wife called before he nodded out. She could tell from his voice that something was wrong, drove over to his house, and found Peter unconscious on the floor, foaming at the mouth. He was just about dead and the paramedics had to use a fibrillator to get his heart going again. The process left six little permanent burn marks on his chest.

Peter moved to Palm Springs after that experience and later found Christ. He ultimately beat his drug habit and moved to the San Fernando Valley. He earned his living as a salesman but also worked with local churches in Thousand Oaks and Palm Springs. That's how he came to learn of Rosey's AYC organization. And when he went to work for Rosey, that was his first real exposure to black people.

We both tried to overcome our relative inexperience with one another's culture by talking things out. Nevertheless, the pressure began to build as a number of my black friends and acquaintances registered their disapproval of our proposed union. Angel's father, Jerry, was the first one to weigh in: "You're going to let a white man raise my kid?" Then Horace, who had been working for me for a year on the distribution of my magazine, threw a fit when he found out. I didn't know if it was because I was marrying a white guy or because I was marrying someone other than him.

My family was mostly relieved when they heard the news. Knowing my background, everybody thought, "Wow, she's finally settling down." My mother may have been a little disappointed that Peter was white. My father didn't mind because he had a brother who married a white French woman.

My mother's side still has a lot of their southern ways and they're suspicious of white people. If I ever complained about Peter, they would always jump in and say, "That's what you get for marrying that white boy." Though they'd always say right away the remark was a joke, I knew otherwise.

I don't believe my two brothers like Peter. He's very strict and I think that offends them. Vera gets along with him and my older sister, Avis, doesn't appear to care about him one way or another.

As the wedding day approached, Peter suggested we separate completely for thirty days and fast for the entire period. He felt we both needed to think about the decision to marry apart from one another. There were to be no calls, no contact whatsoever. I drank water and juice for nineteen days and lost fifteen pounds. Then I broke the fast and had some food. Peter somehow stuck to it for the entire thirty days.

It was during this period that a group of my friends, including Diane, tried to persuade me to change my mind about Peter. Diane had been all for it but when she decided I was acting nonchalant about the wedding, she thought I wasn't taking it seriously.

"You don't know him well enough," she told me.

I said, "What's to know? We meet, we marry, and then adapt and grow." I knew we were going to grow and become different people anyway.

A couple of other friends were saying, "You're crazy. He

doesn't have a steady job, he's white. You should go for your career." Another said, "If you marry white, he'd better be rich." That's how some blacks feel.

They all wondered, "Why would you marry a white guy?" I said, "Because he was the first man to ask me."

Inside, I was thinking, "I'm twenty-eight. What am I going to do? Wait the rest of my life for a black man to ask? Tell Peter he is the wrong color?"

Our thirty-day separation was good timing for a lot of reasons. Peter was busy with a major AYC crusade and I had my business to run. Then about a week before the wedding, Peter and I got into an argument. Angel had an ear infection and was very sick. On the twenty-eighth day of our separation, I called him on the phone to ask him what to do. I could tell he was angry that I had broken the separation vow.

"It's an emergency," I said. "I'm taking her to the hospital."

Peter snapped back, "No, give her two aspirin, say a prayer, and put her to bed."

Peter is a believer in divine healing and feels you should give God a chance to cure you before going to see a doctor. I disagreed. As a mother, my first priority had to be my daughter. If I felt she needed to go to the hospital, she went.

At first, I didn't see it as a big deal. I was independent enough to make those decisions myself. The doctor ended up prescribing an antibiotic—amoxicillin. When Diane heard about Peter's reaction, she was livid. "Are you serious about marrying a man who doesn't believe in doctors or going to the hospital? The man would have let her die," she said. So for the next few days, I heard all this from a woman who'd been divorced twice and was in the middle of a big custody fight with one of her ex-husbands, but I wasn't thinking about that.

The AYC crusade was scheduled for the last weekend in February at the Olympic Auditorium in downtown Los Angeles—just a week before the wedding. On a Friday night,

I walked up to Peter in front of a group of people and told him it was off. I said, "You're insensitive, you don't care about children, and if you don't care about them, I'm not marrying you." All these people were staring at us, and Peter said in a perfectly calm voice, "Okay."

I went home and on Sunday he called. He said, "I've given this a lot of thought. We're getting married next week and it's up to you and God as to whether our wedding is still on." He also said he would be very hurt emotionally if we canceled our plans. On Monday I called him back and told him I wanted to marry him. I put our disagreement down to the basic differences between men and women. We were fasting and hadn't talked in almost thirty days and he wasn't with me to see how sick Angel was.

When I get angry, I'm a screamer and yeller. I realized one of Peter's best attributes was that he was a stabilizing influence on me. He's more rational under pressure and I think being fifteen years my senior has something to do with that. Some of my friends thought he was too old and would cramp my style. Well, I had got the partying out of my system long ago. What I needed was someone to keep me home. It would be a big change, and a welcome change.

During that delicate time, I thought back to something Rosey had told us a couple of months earlier: Once you get married, don't listen to your friends anymore. Many friends and in-laws advise out of their own experiences. Unless they have a special anointing, they shouldn't get involved. When there's a big decision to make, you go to your elders. For us, that was Rosey.

The Tuesday before our wedding, Peter and I had plans to visit a friend for dinner. When we arrived at his house, I opened the front door and was greeted by thirty of my girlfriends. "Surprise!" they yelled. Peter had planned a wonderful bridal shower.

We had talked about keeping our wedding casual and low-key. We actually considered getting married in blue jeans at Rosey's center, and then going out into the neighborhood to do some street witnessing, since that's what we always did on Saturdays at AYC. But a friend of mine named Jerri had been pushing me to wear a dress. "I can't afford it," I told her. She said, "Star, then I'll make you one."

And she did—a beautiful, knee-length, white lace, one-shoulder dress. Some of our other friends got together behind our backs and organized a nice reception, complete with balloons and a cake.

On our wedding day at the AYC, Rosey wore a traditional minister's robe as he delivered the vows in a large classroom jammed with friends and family. We didn't have any money to spend on invitations, but we still managed to draw more than a hundred guests. My mother flew in from New Jersey and my sister Avis and her son David came in from Colorado to attend the ceremony.

Our friends created a matrimonial setting by constructing a makeshift altar and surrounding it with flowers. All the decor—from the balloons right down to the paper plates and cups—was in black and white. That became the trademark for Peter and me. Put us in a room together and you get a nice combined shade of mocha, and it looks real good!

After the ceremony, my mother, Avis, and Angel went to Disneyland. They invited us along but Peter and I had other plans. We hopped in my Peugeot and drove to Santa Monica, where we spent a romantic night in the bridal suite of a luxurious beachside hotel.

By Monday, I was back to work on the magazine and Peter was moving his things into my apartment from his place in Thousand Oaks. Boy, did we have some adjustments to make. One of the first things I made Peter do was rent a video of Alex Haley's *Roots.* He had an awful lot to learn about black history in a very short amount of time, and what better way to do this than watch videos. I believe one of the things that enabled us to make our relationship work was that neither of us was particularly close to our family. Because we were both so independent and stubborn, we couldn't care less about what other people thought of us. That allowed us to resist any pressure from outsiders who hinted we weren't right for each other.

The summer after we got married, I got a call from Vera, and the news was shattering. My parents were getting divorced after thirty-six years of marriage. I was shocked because I wasn't aware that their relationship was falling apart during my years in Los Angeles. I was optimistic enough to believe they could work it out if they just stayed together and communicated what was on their minds, but talking things out was never one of their strong points. I called my mother and said, "You can't do this!" I was floored. After all my years of carefree living, I was finally settling down and recognizing marriage for the sacred covenant it represents. Just as my life was coming together, theirs was falling apart. But there was no changing my mother's mind.

My father always told me, "Never quit, losers quit." I finally understood what he had meant by that, and now he and my mother appeared to be giving up without a fight.

My parents were never very affectionate toward one another and I rarely saw them kiss or hug. As a child, I thought that was the normal way married people conducted a relationship. So I came to believe that love is just a basic commitment couples share for one another. Passion was saved for the characters in the movies.

I presumed that during their thirty-six years together, they had to endure many more challenges than whatever issues had led up to this divorce. I told both of them, "You're in the prime of your life and you're throwing away your entire relationship." I could not believe any issue couldn't be worked out unless it involved domestic violence. They both said they had just grown apart.

In retaliation, I cut them both off for several months. I didn't call them and they didn't call me. I had to admit I was hurting because I had lost my security blanket. Our roles were reversing, and rather than each of them being there for one another in their final years, my brothers, sisters, and I would have to be there for each of them separately.

In early 1986, AYC lost some funding and Peter's salary was reduced to $150 a week. We talked it over and decided he should resign and come to work for me. So we lived and worked together under the same roof, and battled over who was in charge, yet the magazine managed to grow. When we entered our third year of operation, we were paying a secretary and had three commissioned sales reps working for us.

That year, the Internal Revenue Service did a random audit of the magazine. It took them weeks to go through my paperwork and they wanted documentation for every expense I ever listed. After finding no wrongdoing, they dismissed me with a simple "Thanks, see you later." I was so angry. The joke of it was that my three-year gross revenues were just under $200,000. About half of that covered salaries for myself, Peter, a secretary, a distribution man, and our sales reps; the rest covered printing costs and other expenses. Because our overhead was so high, Peter and I were barely getting by. I bet the bureaucrat who showed up to sift through my records took home more than we made. To me, a random audit is an invasion of privacy, particularly when you're treated as guilty until proven innocent.

By 1988, we had set our sights on moving the magazine out of our two-bedroom apartment on Ardmore Street and into a small office on South Oxford Street near Wilshire Boulevard. That spring, however, I started feeling very sick and discovered I was pregnant again. During our first three years of marriage, Peter and I had rarely discussed having children; our magazine was "our baby." That was no exaggeration since we invested every ounce of energy into our jobs and raising Angel. For years, in order to reach our bedroom from the kitchen, we had to wade through a maze of office furniture, an offset printer, and a typesetting machine. Our physical setup didn't leave much room for another child, but that all became irrelevant once I discovered I was pregnant. It was not an accident. Peter and I had decided to go for a baby but I had gotten so busy with the magazine, I had forgotten that we had sex on a day that I was most likely to be fertile.

During this pregnancy, I was more careful about how I took care of my body. Peter encouraged me to get prenatal care and reminded me to keep my appointments. He made sure I was eating right and taking the proper vitamins. In my case, being married certainly made me more responsible for the baby I was carrying. That's why today I encourage young pregnant women to marry so they can avoid going through pregnancy and childrearing alone.

I gave birth naturally to Rachel at UCLA Medical Center on October 23, 1988. I returned to UCLA because I really liked the way the doctors had handled my first birth. I worked right up until I went into labor and spent only one night in the hospital. There were no complications, except in choosing a name. You see, Peter was convinced all along we were going to have a boy so we called the baby Elijah during the pregnancy. Then when a baby girl arrived, we weren't prepared to name her. Angel then suggested Rachel, because there was an "el" in that name, too. Peter liked the name Sarah because in the Bible, Sarah was a good wife to Abraham. Rachel means "gentle" and Sarah means "princess" in Hebrew, and we thought "gentle princess" had a nice ring to it—so Rachel Sarah it was.

Since we didn't have insurance, we made payments to the

hospital to cover the $3,000 bill. That hefty debt was not the reason why I was depressed when I returned home from the hospital. I was upset because we still hadn't moved our business from the apartment to an office. When I walked through the door with Rachel in my arms, there were sales reps in my living room chatting on the phone and using the computer. With two children, I really wanted a home life, and so I turned to Peter and said enough is enough.

Two months later, we finally were able to scrape together the cash to rent the office in the South Oxford building we had been eyeing for months. We agreed to the rent of $1,200 a month, and took out a lease in January 1989. Though the space was only 800 feet square, it allowed us to have some semblance of a home life. For that, I was eternally grateful.

10

THE LOS ANGELES
RIOTS END MY DREAM

On April 29, 1992, I had a meeting scheduled at my office with some parents and two attorneys from the Institute of Justice. They were suing the California Board of Education on behalf of myself and twenty-five other parents who were contending the state had denied our children the constitutional right to an equal education. Our goal was to force the state to give us vouchers so we could educate our kids at private schools.

That day, my daughter Angel and I got our hair and nails done in Westwood, then I dropped her off at a studio for a modeling shoot. My firstborn was growing up fast. She would be turning twelve in October and I had enrolled her in the Barbizon School so she could learn some personal etiquette and how to carry herself with poise and confidence.

I headed into the office to wait for the attorneys and parents to arrive. In eight years, we had built the magazine into a sixty-four-page monthly. Revenues were now $180,000 annually and our company occupied a fifth-floor office suite in Inglewood, not far from the Great Western Forum, home of the Los Angeles Lakers. Our 1,800-square-foot space included a conference room and seven offices for Peter, myself, and our seven full-time employees on the payroll.

My interests had expanded into local politics, and I was particularly concerned with education since my oldest daughter was now a seventh grader and my youngest would be entering kindergarten in less than two years. In early 1992, I worked for a ballot initiative that would have allowed parents like myself who preferred a private education to use state-funded school vouchers to pay the tuition bill. That initiative eventually lost when it was put to the voters, but the defeat didn't sour my interest in education and politics.

The school vouchers meeting was scheduled to begin late in the afternoon, but only a few people showed up. When I turned on the TV, I found out why. The Rodney King verdicts had come down, and all of the police officers accused in the beating had been acquitted. The jury had hung on some of the charges, but that didn't matter: there was immense trouble brewing in Los Angeles.

Like thousands of other folks that day, I sat glued to the television, shocked and hypnotized as a group of black kids dragged a white man with long blond hair from his truck and assaulted him with everything from a hammer to a brick. It was Reginald O. Denny. This was happening at Florence and Normandie Avenues in South Central, a mile or so from where I sat in my office.

Suddenly, it hit me. The two lawyers coming from the Institute were traveling from downtown. They were white and would have to come through South Central. I was frantic until they finally showed up. Their car had been stoned and nearly overturned as it made its way to my office. The irony behind it was that one of the white lawyers had just resigned from a position as a federal prosecutor investigating police harassment and brutality.

We cut the meeting short and I led my visitors back

downtown to their hotel, but not from the direction they came. We took separate cars and drove west—away from the rioting—to the San Diego Freeway. Then we drove north to the Santa Monica Freeway and subsequently east. As I watched the horizon fill with trails of black smoke from fires being lit around Los Angeles, I thought to myself, "Lord, *what* is going to happen to my business?"

We left South Central behind us, but as I was driving along the freeway, I could hear the screaming sirens of emergency vehicles and police helicopters buzzing over my head. I wondered whether the rioting was spreading, and got my answer when I exited at Western Avenue near the First AME church. It was early evening and the street was crowded with blacks who had attended a meeting there. All evening long, blacks were gathering in Los Angeles to vent their frustration over the acquittals of the police who beat Rodney King. I took a left off the ramp and drove north on Western toward Koreatown. One block ahead, I saw smoke pouring from a liquor store. The next thing I knew, fire trucks were speeding down the street straight toward me, and then I heard a popping noise. Somebody was shooting at the fire engines.

I pulled over in front of a McDonald's restaurant and ducked down in my Grand Am to avoid the bullets. As they flew over my head, I knew I wasn't a target because of the color of my skin. Rather, I felt like an innocent bystander caught in the cross fire of a gang shootout. I could smell the smoke and hear the panicked screams of people over the blaring sirens. I buried my face in the front seat of my car, and all I could think about was where my daughters were. I knew Angel was safe at the modeling studio, but I didn't know if my husband had picked up Rachel at a friend's house. I prayed he had, because I knew it would not be safe on the street for my white husband or my racially mixed daughter.

It wasn't so much that people had gone crazy in South

Central that day. I viewed the rioters as the products of the Great Society who were now turning on liberalism. After three decades of handouts, they had not developed the skills to make it on their own. Instead, they had evolved into a group of government-dependent, out-of-control, racist monsters, modern-day urban Frankensteins who burn, beat and shoot when things don't go their way.

After the shooting stopped, I gathered myself, wiped my watering eyes, and started my drive home. When I arrived, I first thanked God that my family was safe and then I turned on the TV and started watching the riots play out their ugly spectacle. I had lived in Los Angeles sixteen years and knew almost every business and its practices. It became clear the rioters were targeting certain retail stores known for not hiring blacks, except on the lowest levels. But it really started to hurt me personally when the rioters appeared to burn indiscriminately. Through the night, I watched several of my advertisers' businesses erupt in flames on television. I saw B&B Records burning and I thought, "Oh my goodness, they owe me money." That selfish thought was quickly replaced by feelings of sadness. I watched other clients burn, Paul's Southwest Camera Shop and Nat Diamond's furniture store. These stores had been with my magazine five years and they had served South Central thirty and sixty years, respectively. Now they were being burned to ashes.

Korean-owned businesses were also being targeted. Their owners had replaced many of the black merchants who had left South Central, and a cultural gap had formed between the Asian proprietors and their black customers. There was a severe language barrier and resentment toward the Koreans, who tended only to hire within their families and their race. Tensions got even worse when a local judge gave a light sentence to a Korean grocer who shot and killed a black teenager named Latasha Harlins.

There was tremendous discord between our two races, but I viewed the Koreans as proud and hard-working people. Many of their stores were distributing my magazine, and I had learned that if you made an effort to learn a little about their culture, the barriers disappeared. I always tried to greet the Koreans in their language, *"Annyong haseyo?"*

As a community of blacks, we weren't making those efforts. Some black businessmen had closed up shop because they got sick of being robbed and harassed. Many residents wouldn't even spend their money in their own neighborhood, preferring instead to do their business at the outlying suburban shopping malls. The Koreans had come in and tried opening up small businesses, but many were chased out even before the rioting began. As South Central burned, I kept wondering who would now risk providing goods and services to residents of the poor neighborhoods affected by the riots.

On the second day of the mayhem, I called a friend in south Orange County who agreed to take in Angel and Rachel until things calmed down. Since January, Peter had been studying at a Charismatic Episcopal church in San Clemente, and fortunately we knew people there. On our way out of the city, we drove through South Central to get a firsthand look at the devastation. I didn't have to go that far because one block from our home, a half dozen local shops had been burned and looted. Four of my suits went up in flames along with the local dry cleaners I patronized. Sitting atop the Baskin-Robbins, where we often went for an after-dinner ice-cream cone, were three Korean men armed with rifles and casting a wary eye on the traffic below. The National Guard, meanwhile, was setting up its post in the parking lot of my grocery store.

COPS VERSUS ROBBERS—WHO'S BAD?

During the ninety-minute drive south, I thought about the beating of Rodney King. He was wrong for taking the police on a high-speed chase and resisting arrest after they finally pulled him over. But those police officers were wrong too, and as long as there are white police officers who feel compelled to brutalize blacks and other minorities when the opportunity presents itself, any progress toward racial harmony, justice for all, and equal opportunity will be thwarted and tensions exacerbated.

I'm aware cops have a tough job, and they can get frustrated when they arrest criminals one day only to see them back out on the street in a short time committing the same crimes. They're under enormous stress and are dealing with criminals in a time when people are showing a lack of respect for authority figures as never before.

As a reformed delinquent myself, I know a little something about that. Looking back, I certainly can sympathize with my own parents and teachers who had no luck at reining in my antisocial behavior. I didn't clean up my own act until I had a child and started going to church and maturing as a human being. In those transition years, I got off welfare, started a business, and raised two daughters, and in the process developed a conservative moral code that I didn't have before. I also started seeing police officers more as friends of law-abiding citizens than as the enemy.

Young people today are being hit from all sides by all sorts of immoral influences, just as I was when I was growing up. Without strong parents, teachers, and clergy to provide some direction, it's no wonder so many of our children are getting away from us and reacting to setbacks like the Rodney King verdicts like trigger-happy gunmen from the Wild West. Something has to be done about rogue cops, but something also has to be done about the moral decline of this nation.

GOOD-BYE BUSINESS

South Orange County is only a short distance from South Central Los Angeles but it seems like another place in time. It's a virtually all-white, conservative enclave. When we arrived in San Clemente and stopped at a restaurant, Peter parked our car and I went inside with the children. As soon as we walked in to get a table, I could feel the eyes of most of the diners on us. What were they thinking? Might they be scared of me and my daughters because we were black and there was still rioting going on up north?

But all the people were actually smiling. Our relief at getting away must have been written all over our faces. Suddenly, I just lost it and started to cry.

After dropping off the kids at my friend's house, Peter and I returned to Los Angeles to check over our offices and find out how our advertisers fared. Our offices were fine. Somebody had put up a "black-owned" sign on the building and we were spared. But most of our clients weren't as fortunate.

Since 1984, I had advertised over five hundred businesses in the magazine. Howell's Bakery had been with me eight years. His business didn't burn but his plaza did. We had seventy-five Korean stores distributing our magazine in South Central and about half of them were burned to the ground. Many of the owners of those that were spared packed their bags and weren't ever coming back.

The month before the riots, we had deposited $18,000 in

advertising revenue. The month after, we banked only $2,000. I had deposited $2,000 the first month I was in business eight years earlier, and now I was right back where I had started.

Yet how did our traditional civil rights leaders react? Did they rally around the businessmen who had lost everything they owned? One afternoon after the riots, I turned on the news and saw that Los Angeles congresswoman Maxine Waters had taken some of those rioting gangsters to Washington, D.C. She went on television and justified the violence and mayhem, calling these young thugs victims of racism. When Jesse Jackson had come out to take a look at the destruction, his excuse was "Desperate people do desperate things." What he really meant was that it was not the rioters who caused the devastation, but "The Man."

Reverend Jackson and Representative Waters decided that the solution to the chaos was to create some government jobs for these hoodlums. Meanwhile, I as a small business person had to shut down my magazine and lay off good, honest, hardworking people who did not go out looting and burning at the first sign of disorder. I had seven employees and eventually had to let five of them go. My husband and number one salesman were white and they couldn't work in South Central until things cooled off. My printer packed his bags and left LA because he was practically destroyed. Most businesses shut down for at least a week and some never reopened. Our magazine had taken a huge blow, but Peter and I were determined to keep publishing.

I was angry, and I vowed not to stay silent as the liberals attempted to turn the riots into another reason to fill black neighborhoods with more social programs for hoodlums.

Three weeks after the riots, I went into action. On May 19, Vice President Dan Quayle gave his famous "Murphy Brown" speech at the Commonwealth Club in San Francisco. That morning, I was on my way to Palm Springs to attend a

Republican fund-raiser where Vice President Quayle was scheduled to appear later in the afternoon. It was there that I got a chance to see a copy of the speech myself. I felt it was "right on"!

What hit home to me was Quayle's point that some of the causes of the Los Angeles riots included a breakdown of the family structure and the reluctance of people to take personal responsibility for their own lives. The poor, he said, were corrupted by a "welfare ethos" that had replaced self-reliance and aspirations to achieve the American Dream. Among other proposals, he suggested reforms that placed time limits on receiving welfare benefits and required participants to work or go to school. He added that absentee fathers had to pay up and return to their families.

Of course, all the attention was focused on the part of the Quayle speech that criticized the *Murphy Brown* television show for glorifying single motherhood. But I agreed with the vice president. Murphy Brown was doing no favors for poor American women. Dan Quayle said it all in his speech: 33.4 percent of all families headed by single mothers are living in poverty. Moreover, two thirds of adult black women are single parents and most are impoverished as well. Their lives don't resemble that of Murphy Brown, a network news anchor who lived in a townhouse and could afford to hire her handyman as a full-time nanny.

Shortly after the Quayle speech, I was discussing my views with Steve Sheldon of the Traditional Values Coalition. He said, "Star, you have a message that needs to be heard." He asked if he could fax some press releases with some of my statements. I said "Go ahead," and the phone hasn't stopped ringing since.

One of the first things I did was debate a white feminist on a local Los Angeles television news show. A prominent local black female TV reporter, Pat Harvey, served as the moderator. Cozying up to me before we went on the air, Harvey said of

Quayle, "I can't believe he said those things." I felt like saying, "Baby, don't judge a book by its cover." Once the debate started, I complimented Quayle and I could tell from the expression on Pat's face that she couldn't believe what was happening: a black female conservative coming of age right before her eyes.

11

GETTING OUT OF TROUBLE

Four months after the riots, we moved to a rental house in South Orange County. Peter was attending a seminary at St. Michael's and the parish bishop, Randy Adler, helped us relocate. He had known Peter since 1988 when Peter was participating in abortion clinic protests with Operation Rescue. Two leaders of the St. Michael's congregation, Father Dan Sharp and his wife Priscilla, mentioned to us that a three-bedroom yellow stucco house next door to them was for rent. It was a perfect size for my family and the location was grand—walking distance to the beach in a nice middle-class neighborhood. We became good friends of the Sharps, who were gregarious white Texans with an affinity for southern cooking. It was a learning experience for me because I hadn't lived near so many white people since childhood. But we had no trouble winning over the Sharps. One morning as I was cooking a meal of liver, onions, black-eyed peas, collard greens, and grits on my stove, Dan smelled the aroma as it filtered out of my kitchen window. I could do no wrong after that.

Though we were strapped financially, I was able to enroll Angel in a private school run by St. Michael's Church. Peter and I continued working in Los Angeles in an effort to salvage what was left of the magazine. Each morning, we drove north on the San Diego Freeway, dropping Rachel off at a private parochial school in South Central before heading into our office.

Our business was fading fast. I met a lot of business owners like us who were struggling financially after the riots. In many cases, it was the husband who was left jobless because his business had been burned out; the wife went to work full-time. Some of those folks are still unemployed.

Peter and I were at our wits' end. It had been nine years since I wrote my social worker that I was quitting the county, and I had no intention of being rescued by welfare again. But Lord, what were we going to do if our business didn't bounce back from the riots?

To stay afloat, we laid off staff and renegotiated all the leases for our phones and office space. Wells Fargo Bank, which handled one of our credit lines, even called and told us, "Based on our records you're in riot territory, so you don't have to pay anything for three months." That seemed cool by me.

We requested payment deferrals from all of our creditors, and many of them gave us a break. I borrowed money from everyone: $10,000 from my dentist, who was an advertiser, and $5,000 from my Aunt Stella. By moving out of our building in Inglewood and leasing two office suites near Los Angeles International Airport for $500 a month, we saved $300 a month on rent. Office space was cheap because commercial vacancy rates soared after the riots. Even with all these cutbacks, the debts kept mounting. For instance, we had to hire a new printer, increasing that outlay by $1,500 a month. In time, we stopped printing monthly; we could afford to do the magazine only every three months or so, and even that was a struggle. We hung on—barely.

Fortunately for my family, I began planning to make a transition away from the magazine after the move from Los Angeles. When things started getting tough after the riots, I eased up on promoting the magazine and began marketing myself. I was a black businesswoman whose views differed dramatically from the traditional civil rights leaders. While there were a lot of black conservatives out there, not many had the gumption to step forward and speak their mind on the issues.

When *USA Today* called in June 1992 to quote a working mother for a school choice article, I gladly gave them an interview. Later that summer, when the *Jane Whitney Show* needed a former welfare mother to say that single motherhood should not be the family structure of choice, I agreed to be a guest on that show. During the riots, I saw firsthand what a bunch of undisciplined young people could do to a community. I got a lot of flak from the studio audience, some of whom felt that Americans should be content to support broken homes and single-parent households, I suppose to ensure that power-hungry feminists had the freedom to go through life manless. I beg to differ!

That summer I also decided to expand an organization I had formed two years earlier, the Coalition on Urban Affairs. It had begun as an information clearinghouse on issues dealing with entrepreneurship, education, and social policy for the pastors and businessmen I had worked with while publishing my magazine. Now I wanted it to become a place for the media and public policy groups to receive a black conservative response to a whole slate of urban issues, ranging from gun control to small business deregulation.

There had to be a place for the part of the black community that didn't sympathize with the rioters who destroyed Los

Angeles in the aftermath of the Rodney King trial. "Wait a minute," they were saying, "those rioters aren't representative of black thinking. This is not our culture." Those were the voices I wanted to be heard!

Today, the Coalition on Urban Affairs advances proposals that include private-sector involvement in treating urban ills. We didn't need any more think tanks or research centers in Washington, D.C. What was needed was the black conservative voice in the inner city.

To promote the organization, I had been visiting churches and schools in Los Angeles to express my conservative views. It was the same thing I had been doing through my magazine, only now I was saying it out loud rather than putting it down on a printed page.

South Central was my baby. I knew about a hundred pastors and dozens of organizations of businesses and private school administrators. When those church leaders needed to make sense out of the increase in homelessness, illiteracy, crime, or welfare, I helped get them before public policy makers so they could get the background to inform their congregations. I also began hosting more social policy seminars and invited national speakers like 1996 presidential candidate Alan Keyes and Oklahoma congressman J. C. Watts to speak at their churches, in addition to local leaders like Rosey Grier and Ron Thigpen, a vice president at Family Savings Bank. Peter took over many of the publishing responsibilities so I could make more time to work on coalition projects.

Remembering what my dad always told me, "Talkers rule the world," I suppose I was eventually destined to start a radio career. Before the riots, I was a periodic call-in guest on KKLA's *Live from Los Angeles*, a Christian talk radio show. I talked about social and cultural issues from a conservative perspective. Then when the violence broke out on April 29, I was on every day analyzing what was happening in the inner city. After things settled down, I resumed calling in to give a biweekly urban update.

In November 1993, the general manager of KGER-AM heard me talking on the radio one day and invited me to sit in for a week on the station's four P.M. to six P.M. show. This was politics with a Christian format, too. Well, general managers track your popularity by the number of callers you generate, and the phone lines just exploded. We sparked some interest out there, and they kept me on as a cohost after the week was up. Within a month, I was cohosting the show full-time. Immediately, I worked out a deal with the station to get my magazine advertisers to buy airtime on my show because I knew my magazine's days were numbered.

THE MAN WHO SHOULD BE PRESIDENT

The month I went to work for KGER, I also received the invitation to speak at Pat Buchanan's conference on New Conservatism, which I wrote about in Chapter 1 of this book. Shortly thereafter, I was asked to contribute to a policy paper on the state of black America. It was sponsored by the National Center for Public Policy Research and they called it Project 21. The report was published to coincide with the liberal Urban League's annual paper on the same subject.

On January 5, 1994, I was in Washington, D.C., participating in a televised press conference on C-SPAN with a large group of black conservatives to announce the findings of the report. After listening to us criticize the traditional civil rights leadership, a black journalist wanted to know how they had let down the African-American community. No one budged, so I stepped up to the microphone and gave an answer: "Blacks were denied from holding public office for so many years," I said, "that once they got into power, black voters felt so much pride they didn't want to let them go. We forgot to hold them accountable for what they were doing."

One of the people who happened to be watching C-SPAN that day was Rush Limbaugh. And on his syndicated TV show, he aired the portion of the press conference in which I spoke, which resulted in a flood of calls from my friends. I was certainly flattered, but didn't think much more about it until a month later when America's most popular talk radio host called me himself. I was out grocery shopping and when I returned, my husband nonchalantly asked, "Guess who called today?" Of course, even after twenty-something hints, I still couldn't figure it out. Finally he fessed up that Rush wanted to interview me for his national newsletter.

The next day, Rush called back and I got to speak with him. He conveyed to me that he was curious about the black conservative movement. I explained to Rush, "For many blacks, there's a real pull between color and conservatism, because you don't want to be labeled disloyal to your color."

Rush disagreed. "But a vote is a private thing."

"It isn't," I answered. "Not with our people it isn't."

I went on to talk about the liberal policymakers. In my mind, it's they who are the racists because they relegated us to accepting handouts and government dependency. Yet liberals have been getting away with calling Republicans racists for so long that many blacks feel racism is now synonymous with the GOP. So I said to Rush, "It's our liberal legislators who have sold us into a type of government-dependent slavery and socialism that is almost unbreakable now.

"The word on the street," I went on, "is that Jesse and all the other black politicians on the left make their money by doing three things: keep blacks voting Democrat; keep them ignorant so they don't step out of the Democratic line; and make liberal Democrats look good in public."

In retrospect, that may have been an outrageous statement

at the time, but I was onto something and so was the rest of black America. The Million Man March, which was still almost two years away, ultimately demonstrated just how much the traditional black leadership had lost its grip on the black race.

During our interview, Rush made a valid point when he noted that "the giant civil rights coalition of this country exists by virtue of the Democratic Party's good graces." He said to me, "The deal is exactly what you said: Deliver black votes in any election to the Democratic candidates, and in exchange we'll give you a bit of a power base."

Rush then made another astute observation: "If too many blacks become self-reliant, self-sufficient, there's no need for Jesse Jackson making the case that they're oppressed; so he's out of a job."

And there's more to it than that, I explained to Rush. Beyond keeping the poor in their place, liberal black leaders also have spent a lot of time bringing down conservative blacks like Supreme Court Justice Clarence Thomas. The motive is that liberals fear blacks like Justice Thomas and retired General Colin Powell because they're successful, conservative, and don't support the welfare status quo. That school of thought flies in the face of the liberal propaganda that America is a racist society hell-bent on denying people of color.

So Rush then asked me, "Is there as much racism in this country as some say there is?"

I responded, "If someone asked me straight out, is America racist? I'd have to say no, Rush, because America offers opportunity for anybody. I don't care where you are or who you are. Even if people of another culture, color, or economic status don't respect you, they can't stop you from being successful.

"Capitalism doesn't have any racial boundaries," I told Rush. "We bind ourselves up in that. When you can go to school and it's free, I don't understand all this 'Racism keeps me back' stuff."

We talked for over an hour and I got off the phone thinking, I like this guy, not because of what he's accomplished, but because of his character and ideas. We really connected.

At the end of our conversation, I mentioned that my views don't exactly put me in the mainstream of black opinion. He said not to worry—that I have more friends who think like I do than I realize. I knew he meant it and that he was one of them.

The next morning I was working at home and my office was suddenly inundated with calls. Rush had gone on his radio show that morning and said, "I just had this most stimulating conversation with this lady, Star Parker, and I'm gonna tell you, she's one of the most intelligent women I've ever met." So my first thoughts were, "Gosh, Rush must not know many women."

For weeks, my friends were kidding me about this, demanding "great wisdom from your highness." The article on me in Rush's March 1994 newsletter generated 2,000 pieces of mail to my office. People just started sending money to the Coalition on Urban Affairs. Folks were calling like crazy and I had to set up three more phone lines just to take messages.

A lot of calls were coming from white people who couldn't believe that what they had read was coming from a black woman. It occurred to me that a large segment of the white population is unfamiliar with black conservatism. One of the last things Rush said during our conversation was that there will be times when you think you're winning, and people will say, "Nah, you're not."

"Don't listen to those voices," he urged me.

"No, we're winning," I said. I thanked him for having the courage to say what needed to be said. I know he's been called a "bigot," but many blacks agree with Rush's views, only they're too afraid to side with him. It takes guts to speak his

mind and put up with being labeled a racist—or in my case—
a sellout. In some circles, we won't win any popularity
contests, but all we ask is a chance to offer our views. Hear us
out and even the naysayers will be surprised how much we all
have in common.

THE MAGAZINE FOLDS

The euphoria I felt from being profiled in Rush's newsletter
was short-lived. On a summer day in June 1994, Peter and I
decided to shut down the magazine. Our printing debt alone
was $15,000, and one decade after the start-up, we were in the
hole for $150,000. I wondered, "God managed to deliver me
from welfare; how is he going to help us get out of this." One
dreary morning over coffee, I said to Peter: "We can't keep
going on like this. We've got to stop printing for a while."

By this time, I was bringing in a steady income from my
radio show and I had recently joined a college speaking circuit
with the Young Americans Foundation. Still, I felt sick about
losing my magazine. I had a plan to go national and perhaps
franchise the publication in urban areas across the country. I
wanted to employ hundreds, make millions, and now my
dream had vanished.

With the business gone, Peter was able to return to his
original calling: the ministry. It was a tough transition for
him because he had set aside his own aspirations to help with
the magazine. He was severely depressed at the time, but he
was able to work toward completing his master's degree in
divinity at St. Michael's Charismatic Episcopal Seminary. He
also has been serving as the fund-raising director of St.
Michael's Society, the benevolent arm of our church. As he
had done with Rosey Grier, Peter was working again with the
poor, the homeless, immigrants, and single mothers. He and

Father Joseph, the director of the society, help pay their clients' bills, find them employment, and give them etiquette and job training referrals. It's proof to me that private charities can also be part of the solution to dealing with folks on welfare because charities do things welfare can't, like provide moral guidance to the participants.

My radio work took a turn in 1995 when I left KGER for my own daily radio call-in show in San Francisco on Hot Talk 560 KSFO-AM. I did the show from home, but that job lasted only about nine months, in part because the station wanted me to relocate to the Bay Area. I got another radio job at KMPC in Los Angeles in early 1996, but I think I was a little too brash for them. They canned me after only three months! When I spoke out on issues dealing with homosexuality, like my opposition to states sanctioning homosexual marriages, homosexual activists lobbied to get me off the air and their efforts were rewarded. But there were other factors that led to my firing. I was unhappy at the station because even though the pay was great and the show hours were only noon to three P.M., Monday through Friday, I had my own personality conflicts with management and time constraints that couldn't be resolved. My priority has always been to be available for my kids, and when the station extended my day from ten A.M. to four P.M., I knew it wasn't going to work. My commute was close to three hours round trip because of traffic. I wanted to be home in the morning to make my daughters breakfast and take them to school, and then be home in time to cook them dinner. No job was worth that type of sacrifice to me.

KMPC and I parted ways in June. Since then, I've been working full-time for the Coalition on Urban Affairs and speaking at colleges and universities. I also was hired as a correspondent for GOP television during the Republican National Convention in San Diego.

On the night Nancy Reagan addressed the crowd, I was invited by the GOP to give a speech on the convention floor. I shared my story—that there is life after welfare and a future built on the free market system and a strict moral code.

The convention was truly an awesome affair, and it illustrated just how diverse the Republican Party is. Although we lost this past presidential election, the GOP campaign message of "Unity, Hope and the American Dream" is a slogan the party should promote into the twenty-first century.

The week after the convention, I got a call from the British Broadcasting Company to consult and report on a documentary on black conservatives, which aired last October.

Prior to the convention, I spent part of the summer preparing for the annual Irby family reunion for the weekend of July 19. It was scheduled to take place at my home, so there was much work to be done. We hosted thirty-five of my relatives from around the country, and I took them on a two-day chartered bus tour of Southern California and Tijuana, Mexico. It cost $600 but I had been setting aside money for the reunion for a year. In Los Angeles, we visited the Hollywood Walk of Fame, historical Olvera Street, and Rodeo Drive in Beverly Hills. Everybody wanted to see O. J. Simpson's Brentwood estate, but the bus driver couldn't take us there because the neighborhood was closed off to sightseers. In San Diego, I got to show everyone the GOP convention site. Grandma Warreno made the trip and she kept up with all the young people. She's still as tough as ever.

My father James, now sixty-four, went on to earn a doctorate in education after his Air Force career, but he has since retired from teaching. He continues tutoring students in reading and writing. He also publishes instructional articles in a newsletter he patterned after my magazine. He calls it the *N.F.T.A. Christian Courier* and distributes about five hundred copies a month to churches in Mount Holly, New Jersey. He learned he had lung cancer in 1991, and the doctor gave him only six months to live. He quit his pack-a-day cigarette habit, refused chemotherapy, and chose a treatment of natural herbs and prayer. A most lucky man, he's still here today, God bless him.

My mother, Doris, now sixty-five, lives in a condominium she bought in the town of Upton, New Jersey, about a fifteen-minute drive from my dad's house. She's a self-trained horticulturist and works full-time at a nursery tending flowers. She loves watching sitcoms and game shows on television and is very involved with a local Baptist church.

Avis, now forty-three, is living in Augusta, Georgia, with her son, David, a high school basketball star. She's divorced and currently an Army master sergeant. She plans on retiring very soon after twenty years of service and has her sights set on starting her own business, possibly in real estate. She has asked me to give her some tips on setting it up.

Michael, forty-one, left the Air Force in 1982 after nine years of service. He's now an electrician living in Sacramento with his wife, Brenda, and their daughter and son.

Vera, now thirty-eight, is an accountant but she's switching careers to become a teacher. She has a twenty-one-year-old daughter. A widow, she lives in Travelers Rest, South Carolina, north of Greenville. Living there also is my youngest brother, Eric, thirty-seven, who is a chef at Furman University.

When I see my family, I think of the old crowd from Mount Holly. I've lost touch with Frank, Big Ant, Elijah, and Sabra, and I hope they're doing well because I'll never forget them. My old friend Karen, who came with me to California back in 1976, eventually moved up to the Bay Area to attend college. I heard she went on to a career in hotel management.

My Los Angeles pals have gone their separate ways, too. Leona lost custody of her daughter after she fell victim to drugs, and apparently she's one step from being homeless. Her sister Brenda and her daughter moved to the Central American country of Belize to care for her grandmother's estate. Penny is an office clerk for an insurance company and lives with her daughter in the San Fernando Valley. I still feel a sense of pride that I was able to give her an opportunity to quit welfare once and for all.

The big plus about not having a daily radio job is that I'm able to spend more time with my family. When I did my show in Los Angeles, my commute from south Orange County was about an hour each way. I can spend more time with Rachel, who is now eight and in third grade at St. Michael's school. Angel, sixteen, graduates from high school in the spring of 1997. She has her sights set on the University of California, Irvine.

Her father, Jerry, is attempting to forge a relationship with her. They talk on the phone and he sends her money on occasion. Jerry today is divorced, has a five-year-old son, and makes his home in Los Angeles County. Ironically, he's also in the radio business, working as an announcer.

My one regret about moving to south Orange County is that we weren't able to provide a more stable educational environment for Angel. In the spring of 1993, Angel graduated from eighth grade at St. Michael's and was accepted at Santa Margarita High School for the 1993–94 school year. Our plan was to have her complete high school there since it was one of the best schools in Orange County. Tuition was steep—$400 a month at a time when we were really struggling—yet we decided to make the commitment.

Of the 2,000 students at Santa Margarita, you could count the number of blacks on two hands. In her second semester, I had to have a heart-to-heart talk with Angel, because she had been called a "nigger" at school for the first time in her life. I told her that her other friendships with white kids were much more important than words that came from the mouth of one bigot; that one bad soul out of one hundred should not change your views toward other white people. I told her not to forget the goodness in those friends who came over to our house for a slumber party. You have to realize who you are as a human being, and how many people love you regardless of your color.

The trouble didn't end there. In the summer of 1994, a black classmate of Angel's got beaten up by some white kids—apparently from a rival school. Ruben Vaughn was a six-foot-two freshman who had started for the varsity football team. He was a star and had a lot of girls running after him, including white girls. One day he got invited to a party by a schoolmate, someone outside his circle of friends. When he showed up to the party with some buddies, they were met by twenty-five to thirty white kids who frightened off Ruben's friends and then ganged up on Ruben. They beat him, stabbed him, and broke his jaw and nose.

Word on the street was that some white guy was getting him for dating his sister. It was big news in the local papers, and his father told a reporter that one of his son's friends heard someone shout, "Let's get this nigger," as the assault began.

He didn't come back to Santa Margarita and when Angel returned, there were only two other blacks attending the whole school. What upsets me most about this is that none of the school authorities wanted to admit there was a racial problem. There was never any mention of Ruben's case, as though nothing had ever happened. Angel felt uncomfortable and her grades slipped. When I went to talk to the school deans, I felt they were unresponsive. They probably looked at our file and wrote me off as a "slow-pay" since we were having trouble paying the tuition. I wish I had been able to pay with a school voucher—perhaps that would have given me a little more clout with the school.

After the first semester, I withdrew Angel and enrolled her in our public high school, where she's thriving. Last fall, she was elected by her fellow classmates to become the school's Ethnic Relations Commissioner. I'm proud of her accomplishment, but I think her school goes overboard in dealing with potential racial problems because they're always pulling the minority kids out of class to attend "group tolerance" meetings. It seems to me that the school could put more emphasis on academic achievement and spend less time on social development.

Despite our experience at Angel's old school, living in south Orange County is part of my American Dream. What racism does exist is definitely in the minority because everywhere I go, the people are friendly and kind. Most of my black friends living in the area feel the same way.

Someday, I hope to resurrect my magazine. I believe it's my calling and it provides a service for the black community—a conservative voice emphasizing self-initiative and morality. I have always viewed the magazine as a link between the neighborhoods, the churches, and the businesses in the area, and would like to see it grow so I can offer job training opportunities to young men and women who need that first break.

In the meantime, my coalition is holding seminars for church and business leaders in the black community. Last fall before the November election, I held a conference on the differences between the Republican and Democratic platforms from the coalition's office near Los Angeles International Airport. For my 1997 programs, I expect to recruit some welfare mothers to volunteer to man the display tables and registration desks in the hope that they could network with the pastors and business owners attending my seminars.

These days when I sit in my upstairs den and look out at the Pacific Ocean, as the sun sets behind a cloud and the sky turns from blue to purple to red, I know life will turn out okay—not just because of my faith in God, but because I know there will be a new and better tomorrow. After all, this is America.

PART 2

THE DESTRUCTION OF BLACK AMERICA

The damage to America's inner cities is incalculable, and the responsibility begins with the liberal Democrats, the authors of the Great Society and the War on Poverty. But they did not act alone in the crime they've committed against black Americans. For the past thirty years, scores of civil rights leaders and millions of black men and women have stood by silently as the black community was used as a guinea pig for a grand political experiment to transform our most troubled urban neighborhoods into a model for government socialism. Why didn't we speak out? Why have we smothered dissenting voices that challenge the premise of the Great Society programs that turned much of black America into a welfare state? Perhaps it comes down to inexperience and pride, and a fear today that if we abandon the Democratic Party, who will listen to us then?

PIMPS, WHORES AND WELFARE BRATS

The Pimps: The Democrats Who Got Us in This Mess in the First Place

The political pimps are government socialists who believe man is basically good, but has a few character flaws that can be corrected with a little help from Big Brother. Without government intervention, the pimps don't believe blacks have the smarts or self-initiative to make it on their own. What's more, the pimps insist on the preservation of what they describe as the *permanent underclass*, which they claim is defenseless against the evil influences of capitalism and religion. So the pimps produced numerous social programs for the poor, but excluded religious institutions from the equation.

Political pimps have been around forever, but they made their big push during the civil rights protests of the 1960s. Blacks had endured years of segregation and discrimination under Jim Crow, and as they were breaking free of those shackles, the pimps showed up on the scene and said, "Hey listen, black folks, we'll help you. We'll initiate some new laws like the Voting Rights Act and the Civil Rights Act." It would have been simpler to enforce the Constitution of the United States, such as the part that reads that all men are created equal. But no, the pimps had something better up their sleeves. They were going to take black America for a ride.

Don't get me wrong. The civil rights movement was necessary to rid the land of Jim Crow. Southern blacks were abandoned during post–Civil War Reconstruction because the North did not want to confront the Southern states for implementing apartheid. Instead of confiscating Congressional voting rights, America turned a blind eye that didn't reopen until the civil rights movement of the 1960s. The changes took some time, but Americans black and white said, "Enough is enough," and Jim Crow laws were wiped out.

Assurances of equal opportunity were necessary so we could compete in the marketplace for jobs, but it didn't stop there. Whether the motivation was collective guilt on the part of white power brokers or a desire to redistribute the wealth, or a combination of both, the pimps created a series of social programs with the stated intent of wiping out poverty. Their solutions included food stamps and Aid to Families with Dependent Children, forced school busing, and public housing. They dubbed their agenda "the safety net." I tend to view it all as a giant spider's web.

We know street pimps are opportunists by nature, and when they spot a vacant corner, they move in faster than it takes a hooker to swipe the money from your wallet. So the liberal Democrats made lots of promises to all those civil rights leaders in exchange for delivering the black vote. The pimps told their whores: "We are going to help you get out from under the weight of racism, but you are going to have to sell us your community to experiment with socialism in America."

But we all know pimps don't know how to take care of their whores. What black men and women failed to do after the War on Poverty began was to take stock of what it was doing to our urban centers. They never said, "Now, what have been the effects of all these social programs? Did they turn our neighborhoods into the Great Society Lyndon Johnson once talked about?" There was no critical examination; the pimps were allowed to spin a wider web, creating more programs when something went wrong.

For instance, with the creation of affirmative action in education came the lowering of educational standards for blacks. The pimps' rationale was that they had to fill minority quotas, but since not enough blacks were excelling in school to meet the demand, they increased the supply by lowering college entrance requirements and rewriting the so-called racially biased grading systems and achievement tests. What black folks should have said was, "Hold on, children of all races can learn. Improve our schools and give us some other educational choices. Color doesn't matter."

With affirmative action jobs, doors were opened to black men and women that had once been closed, but nobody gave any thought to the fact that losing our best and brightest young people would destroy the economic base that had sustained our communities for decades.

With forced busing, black children were herded into white schools far from home, supposedly to get an equal education. But it also sent a powerful message to these kids that black neighborhoods didn't have much to offer, even though we have fine private schools.

Year after year, we called on the pimps to take care of us instead of caring for ourselves. "Gimmee more, gimmee more," we said. In essence, it's been just another type of slavery. And all we got to show for thirty years of fighting poverty is two generations of welfare dependents and a younger generation that doesn't give a darn about anything.

The Whores

The pimps had no trouble finding some whores in search of some cash and clout. Plenty of black leaders, inspired by everything from a desire for change to retribution, were more than happy to join in as foot soldiers. They threw their support behind the radical left, making Democratic control of the House of Representatives a lock until 1994.

Their reward was a job in government, a power base in their home district, and plenty of campaign money. Washington got a Congress weighted with liberal extremists. What a joke that turned out to be. It was like making a bargain with the devil. After that, giving away tax dollars to special programs and creating monstrous bureaucracies was the easy part.

The Welfare Brats

The children of the first generation of welfare recipients are a group I call the "welfare brats." These are people who feel life is not worth living without a handout from the Great Society. Instead of sticking by the principles of hard work and self-reliance that brought black Americans up from slavery, they latched on to an attitude that says, "I want it now." They coveted what they could not afford and rebelled.

I was a welfare brat in spirit—even though I was the first in my family to go on AFDC. Is it a far stretch to imagine that since a welfare brat's mother receives government assistance, society is suggesting that mother and child are victims of racism and entitled to handouts? So many welfare brats learn early that lawless behavior is an acceptable response to economic injustice. "You get yours, baby, and I get mine!"

Folks don't want to admit it, but the infection has spread. Now middle-class Americans are catching on to the welfare brat mentality, and they like it. They have bought into this self-destructive culture of dependency as much as any third-generation welfare recipient. They don't want to give up their Social Security, their Medicare, federal college tuition aid, or prized mortgage interest tax deduction. White welfare brats complain out loud, too, except they tend to riot at the ballot box—you know, do things our way or we'll throw you out of office. Many blacks, on the other hand, don't bother voting on election day because they don't feel they can make a difference.

THE BREAKDOWN OF THE BLACK FAMILY

Let's dissect this virus piece by piece. The fundamental theme behind the pimps' agenda is that poverty is intolerable and that no one should be poor. As a result, instead of folks feeling, "I want that and I'm going to work hard to get it," they have been convinced that they're entitled to feel, "I don't have that. I resent you for having it. You should feel guilty for having it, and I'm morally obligated to take it away from you."

So here was the pimps' plan: Redistribute the wealth and eliminate poverty. Sounds terrific. Problem is, the money has to come from somewhere. So taxes rose, the welfare checks were cut, families started falling apart, and taxpayers got fed up.

Families were being shredded on many fronts. In the white community, the pimp feminists went to work on the non-working women: they encouraged them to step out of their traditional roles as homemakers and enter the workforce, putting their kids on the back burner. In the process, a woman's traditional role of staying at home and raising a family was devalued. For a variety of reasons, divorce rates were on the rise, leaving record numbers of single women raising families on their own.

Government welfare policies were adopted that encouraged fathers to leave home so their families could collect benefits. Those policies contributed to the destruction of marriages, and these social and economic changes were catastrophic to blacks. Not only were families breaking up, government "altruism" was replacing the charity role traditionally played by churches, diminishing the importance of religion.

Families and businesses are the nucleus of any community. For blacks, the link to those institutions was the church. Remember, for decades the Bible was the only book blacks were permitted to read, and it provided blacks the moral foundation to raise their families. The church also established many of the major black colleges and universities—Fisk, Spelman, Bethune-Cookman, and Tuskegee.

Let's add it up: The church was in decline, moral decay was on the rise, women began flooding the workforce, the welfare rolls were expanding, and government was promoting the view that there was a permanent underclass that could not survive without government help. It sounds like one grand socialist experiment, and we have the pimps to thank for it.

Now I ask you, what is a more racist point of view—the Republican attitude that says, "Hey, if I can do it, you can do it," or the Democratic viewpoint that says, "We cannot make it without government?"

SPIN CONTROL:
COVERING UP THE BLACK URBAN CRISIS

The pimps and whores have done their job. It seems any time a conservative points out that a disproportionate number of blacks are on AFDC welfare, the immediate response from liberals is that more whites are on welfare than blacks—5.3 million to 5.05 million in 1992, according to recent government statistics.

When conservatives observe that a disproportionate number of nonwhites are getting abortions, the pimps hiss and the whores dismiss the issue by arguing that most abortions are performed on white women—65 percent to 35 percent according to the Alan Guttmacher Institute.

When conservatives cry out that crime is destroying urban neighborhoods, much of it black-on-black crime, these leftist groupies always retort that our criminal justice system is biased against color and that white folks are experiencing high rates of white-collar crime in their own community that is being ignored by authorities.

I don't agree that the black dilemma is merely a reflection of the ills affecting society as a whole. The Heritage Foundation has reported that $5.4 trillion has been spent for the War on Poverty, and I believe another $5 trillion won't change a thing for urban America. Blacks account for 13 percent of the U.S. population, and yet black households comprised 36.6 percent of the AFDC roll in 1993, according to the Department of Health and Human Services. Will another round of spending improve the situation? Doubt it!

This is why: Welfare in the black community has transformed receiving public aid into an alternative lifestyle rather than what it was intended to be, a program to help tide people over in hard times until they could get back on their feet. If you don't believe it, look at the AFDC's own statistics: In 1993, the federal government reported that 47 percent of all the families receiving AFDC that year had been on the roll for twenty-five months or longer. That's not transition. That's dependency, and it trickles down from generation to generation. That's the legacy of the socialist pimp.

I have an unmarried friend named Julie who has five children by the same man, and she has insisted for years that she never needed a job because she could live on the county and stay home with her kids. Now she looks up and sees that both her daughters have babies and collect AFDC welfare, just as she did. One child is fifteen and the other is seventeen.

When those kids were little, she always raved how wonderful welfare was. Now she says, "I don't know what I did wrong." I do—she let government socialism and its Democratic promoters lead her into the welfare abyss.

LEWD LEFTISTS: LIBERALS I HAVE NO USE FOR!

Contrary to popular perception, racism is not the reason for the tension between black and white America; the blame lies with the social programs championed by the pimps and whores—a tandem I would like to categorize as the "lewd left."

I derived this expression from something I read in the Bible in Isaiah 32: 5–6 (King James version). Part of that verse describes how the "vile" person shall no longer be called "liberal," and the passage goes on to say that the vile person makes "empty the soul of the hungry" and "devises wicked things to destroy the poor, even when the needy speaks right," and causes "the drink of the thirsty to fail."

I have come to see liberal social policies as robbing the soul of the poor because those policies are saying that the poor no longer have the ability to fend for themselves and that their minimum-wage jobs are meaningless. Instead of teaching the needy how to utilize their God-given talents, the leftists say we should make them equal by redistributing the wealth. I consider these stereotypes and policies vile, or "lewd."

The consensus in America after the civil rights movement was to work toward bridging racial gaps and assembling a unified nation. But that was not enough for the lewd leftists. They had a larger agenda and decided to piggyback on the civil rights movement, replacing Dr. Martin Luther King's plea for moral accountability with their own cry for moral relativism.

Their legacy is the creation of the liberal social policies that have dominated the Democratic agenda since the late 1960s. Almost thirty years later, the lewd leftists still have firm control of the political tenor of our nation, and during the takeover, they edged God away from the center of our national moral compass. They were like the corporate raiders of the 1980s, and religion was the asset they no longer had any use for. Consequently, many Americans no longer have a relationship with God—a spiritual common denominator that is vital to combat hatred.

Let there be no doubt about who the lewd leftists are supposedly feeling sorry for—blacks and Hispanics. They are selling us the premise that many minorities can't govern their lives and need welfare and free abortion to clean up after their mistakes and failures. They have decided that many foreigners don't have the ability to learn English, and therefore that speaking English should not be a requirement for obtaining U.S. citizenship. Nor should an immigrant's child have to be educated in English, which has led to the creation of bilingual schools. That's not sympathy in my book; it's a presumption that some people are too stupid to learn, and that's racism.

Secular humanists are responsible for creating a world where we are numb to random violence and perverted behavior. By loosening our grip on moral absolutes and values, we have created a time when it seems that virtually no abnormal behavior can be considered out of the ordinary. So instead of punishing outrageous acts, we promote them by sympathizing with criminals because of their deprived upbringing or because they were somehow abused and neglected as children. We don't punish them, or we let them out of prison sooner than they deserve. This attitude—coddling criminal behavior—has made our inner cities lethal places in which to live.

The ACLU

The American Civil Liberties Union is the most destructive special interest group on the American legal scene today. It is the kingpin of political pimps. It's an organization that is rooted in the hatred of capitalism and religion. In his book *Trial and Error*, author George Grant, a leader in the pro-life movement and advocate for the poor and homeless, lays out the ACLU agenda. He quotes ACLU founder Roger Baldwin on the partisan nature of the ACLU's mission: "I am for socialism, disarmament, and ultimately for abolishing the state itself as an instrument of violence and compulsion. I seek social ownership of property, the abolition of the propertied class and sole control by those who produce wealth. Communism is the goal. It all sums up into one single purpose—abolition of the dog-eat-dog world under which we live."

According to Grant's research, back in 1943 the ACLU secured the right for children to refuse to salute the flag or recite the Pledge of Allegiance in public schools. In the 1960s, they successfully argued for the banning of nativity displays, Christmas decorations, and the singing of carols in public schools and on public property. The ACLU also opposes voluntary school prayer. They are secular humanists to the core.

Their extreme ideology endorses the sale of pornography. They oppose sobriety checkpoints, and push for the legalization of drugs. In religion, they want to take away the tax exemption of churches but support the exemption for satanism. In health, they oppose medical safety regulations and reporting, but support abortion on demand. In family issues, they defend polygamy and mandatory sex education and oppose all spousal and parental consent laws related to abortion.

The ACLU even has argued "that teaching monogamous, heterosexual intercourse within marriage is a traditional American value and is an unconstitutional establishment of a religious doctrine" and thus "violates the First Amendment."

This organization is waging a vicious war on our cities and deserves to be banished to Death Valley.

The Media Elites: Flag Bearers of the Lewd Left

Have you read a newspaper lately? It's not hard to believe there's a media conspiracy to promote a biased, secularist world view. Most of the major networks, major daily newspapers, and magazines are run by liberal publishers and editors. *The New York Times*, the *Los Angeles Times*, and *The Washington Post*—the country's most influential news sources—are unabashedly liberal and serve to fan the propaganda of the political pimps. Liberal network anchors (and you know who I'm talkin' about) are equally culpable.

The Watergate scandal had something to do with this. Thousands of young liberal college students—inspired by Woodward and Bernstein—flooded the industry and have profound influence on how most issues are covered by the media today—despite the fact that television viewers and readers are far more conservative on average than the people who report on the subjects they hear and read about.

Kid-glove treatment is given to the likes of Bill and Hillary Clinton, while Newt Gingrich is continually scrutinized. Anita Hill, who screamed foul when conservative Clarence Thomas was nominated for the U.S. Supreme Court, is cast as a champion of women's rights. Paula Jones, who has accused President Clinton of sexual harassment, is passed off as a pathetic opportunist who's distracting the president.

When a television news show needs a black point of view, the call more frequently goes out for Jesse Jackson than for a conservative. The media expects blacks to whine about racial injustice, which is much more telegenic than a black conservative telling an audience that America can work if you give it a chance.

In January 1996, I watched President Clinton's State of the Union address, and after it was over, I couldn't find a conservative commenting on the speech on one major network. Liberals control what we read and what we watch, and for years have been the advance men in the lewd left's drive to control the political agenda. About the only stronghold of conservative thought these days is talk radio. So folks, turn off the TV, throw away the newspapers, and tune in to your local conservative talk radio show. And of course, listen to Rush every day!

THE KILLING OF A RACE

I wish I had given more thought to the four abortions I had. If just one person had said, "Star, what you're doing is wrong," it might have changed the destiny of my life. If abortion had been illegal when I was prancing in and out of those clinics, I probably would have had that baby the first time around and it could have changed my life the way it did three years later when I gave birth to my firstborn, Angel. After that, I might have been more careful about getting pregnant. Just as in my day, there are no consequences for stupid behavior today.

If I had carried my first pregnancy to term, I probably would have gone home to live with my parents, as my mother suggested when I had Angel. I think we need to encourage that more. Parents should welcome their daughters back home in these circumstances because parental responsibility does not end when a child turns eighteen, as it did in my home. Parenting continues forever.

Who needs mom and dad when government has developed a program for every responsibility a lame parent has abdicated, right down to free school breakfasts and lunches?

A government-subsidized abortion is another example of a program set up to rescue irresponsible men and women. I used abortion as birth control and gladly let Medicare foot the bill. One of my friends had eleven abortions gratis—all courtesy of Medicare. That's her right? How do we justify such absurd behavior? President Clinton wants abortion safe, legal, and rare, so I guess she violated the "rare" part. Well, to her, eleven abortions is "rare" because she's got a friend who had fifteen. If the president wants abortion to be rare, he should take every woman coming through those clinic doors and say, "Honey—you need to change your behavior. We need to teach you how to say 'NO!' "

Subsidized Murder

One of my biggest gripes with the pro-abortion movement is that all taxpayers must pay for abortions, even if it goes against their religious beliefs. Consider Planned Parenthood. They want you to think they are performing a vital public service providing low-cost health care to women, but I believe they are committing the crime of the century by slaughtering millions of unborn children.

Lest we forget—Planned Parenthood gets paid handsomely with taxpayers' dollars for conducting legal genocide. Folks, if what it's all about is "the right to choose" and "reproductive rights," why doesn't Planned Parenthood perform those abortions for free, or even at cost? It's my opinion that they are making a huge profit from dead flesh and that is a crime against humanity.

Shame on black ministers who support abortion on demand. Jesse Jackson, just prior to his 1984 presidential bid, shifted his lifelong pro-life position to pro-abortion. He used to oppose abortion because he believed it was a method of racial cleansing. Reverend Jackson, you were right on the first time around. As blacks abort their "unwanted" and "unplanned" children in alarming numbers, our black leaders quietly watch the holocaust from the sidelines, making the same mistake European leaders made when they discovered Germany's final solution and ignored it.

Black America needs to wake up! Statistics show abortion is really destroying us as a people. Statistics from the Alan Guttmacher Institute show that nonwhites account for more than one third of the estimated 1.5 million abortions performed each year. No wonder Planned Parenthood is continually defending it's founder, Margaret Sanger, from charges of racism and allegations that her intentions were darker than her advertised design to provide health care and birth control to poor women.

We Don't Own Our Bodies

The feminist line is that women own their bodies and should be able to do what they want with them, including abort an unborn child. But in truth, we don't own our bodies. If that were the case, we would be able to take illicit drugs and sell ourselves into slavery and prostitution, if that's what we chose.

I see abortion as a human rights issue, not a property issue. I thought the property issue had been settled when we abolished slavery. Remember, black slaves were property and their masters felt they had a right to do whatever they wanted with them. Now abortion advocates are saying that they own their bodies and can treat them however they want, and that goes for the human being inside of them.

Of course, we've seen the logical extension of this mode of thinking: if we own our bodies we should be able to take our own life, even if it requires the help of a second person. Well, people, that's illegal, but jury after jury keeps acquitting Dr. Jack Kevorkian after he hooks up willing patients to his death machine to kill them off under the guise of "physician-assisted suicide." They let him go because the abortion holocaust has dulled our senses.

It's Time for Mom and Dad to Take a Stand

Not only does the lewd left get us to pay for abortions, they also have convinced us in some states that minors should be able to get them without notifying their parents. Where does government get off replacing the role of families? Talk about bumping aside moms and dads. How can parents catch hell for not disciplining their children when a daughter can get an abortion without them ever knowing? Why is it that a minor needs parental consent for any other medical procedure, except an abortion?

Girls, you've got to call home if you're pregnant! And your boyfriends' parents must get involved if we're ever going to cut down on the rate of teen pregnancy in this country. Twenty-five states currently have mandatory parental notification laws for minors considering getting an abortion, but in most of these states the minor girl can get a court order to keep the abortion private. In California, a school nurse can refer a pregnant girl to an abortion clinic without any parental consent, removing the family from the situation altogether.

Families have been stripped of their role in society. Parents are intimidated from saying what needs to be said: "Hey, kids, maybe you should get married, and we can build a relationship between the families and work this thing out together." But these kids think, "Nah, I can't burden my family." Then they head for the nearest abortion clinic.

Sensible Alternatives to Abortion

Plenty of lewd leftists say, "I'm not pro-abortion, I'm pro-choice." Well, how about lending support to some choices that encourage life, and not death. There are other places single pregnant women could turn to besides AFDC welfare and abortion clinics, even if they can't get help from their families or the fathers of their children.

One place could be a group home run by an organization that would teach a young mother responsibility, values, and job skills. If you shifted those welfare dollars going to young mothers into productive private programs specializing in providing them support, out-of-wedlock birth rates could drop dramatically.

I know quite a few couples complaining about taxes who live in large houses. Why couldn't the government offer families hefty tax credits for taking in pregnant girls? These families could talk to young mothers about discipline and love. I have a lot of confidence in the nature of people. If the caretakers treat the mother as part of the family, she's going to learn about taking care and being part of a family.

Thinking About Our Next Generation

The lewd left has infiltrated society to such an extent that even moderate conservatives feel they have to rid our culture of religion and endorse tax-supported abortion or risk being labeled unsympathetic to the poor and minorities. The media pounds this into our skulls day and night, but shouldn't blacks wake up and see that abortion is wiping out our next generation? It's time to get rid of the guilt and start exercising our conscience. You want your own children to lead moral lives and avoid getting pregnant out of wedlock, so why not endorse public policies that reflect that sentiment?

THE WHORES' RALLYING CRY: RACISM

I see it all the time when a black person isn't hired for a particular job, scores poorly on a standardized test, or gets fired. The problem is never the individual's performance. The culprit is always "racism."

I saw it when U.S. Representative Mel Reynolds, of Illinois, was indicted for having sex with a minor. It wasn't a case of a man who was unable to control his urges. Reynolds said he was the victim of a "racist justice system," done in by a girl who was an "emotionally disturbed nut case."

Benjamin Chavis was dismissed as head of the NAACP amid allegations that he used the agency's funds to pay off a woman accusing him of sexual harassment. Who was to blame for his getting canned? "Reactionary African-Americans working with right-wing Jewish groups," he whined.

Same thing when U.S. Representative Walter Tucker, of Compton, California, was indicted for extortion and accepting a bribe. It wasn't another greedy public official getting nabbed with the goods, but another black politician being persecuted because of his race. In every one of these stories, there's always some apologist ready to wave the racist warning flag. "It looks to me like some kind of conspiracy is going on here," Royce Esters, president of the Compton, California, chapter of the National Association for the Advancement of Colored People, said in reaction to the Tucker charges. "Every time you turn around, there's some kind of indictment against a black leader."

The popular sentiment among blacks is that high-profile minorities are attacked by the white justice system because of their color. This was the case with Tucker, who was indicted for crimes he committed while mayor of Compton, California, near Los Angeles. We ignore that he evaded taxes in a black city, accepted bribes in a black city, and committed extortion in a black city. He betrayed the very people who voted for him, and those facts have nothing to do with whites coming to get him. He was a fraud to his own people and caused a lot of pain to the people of Compton.

The Reynolds and Tucker indictments were handed down a week apart in August 1994. Both men were eventually convicted of their respective crimes. They aren't alone. Washington, D.C. mayor Marion Barry, convicted of cocaine possession in 1990, was filmed on video smoking crack cocaine. He argued he was the victim of a prejudiced justice system that persecutes blacks for crimes that whites get away with all the time. As for rapist Tyson, "If he had been white, he would have never served a day on this crime," said the Reverend Wyatt T. Walker, one of the Harlem pastors who tried to stage a Tyson homecoming parade after he was released from prison. Cooler heads prevailed and the celebration was canceled.

All these men belong to the black martyr–racist conspiracy club, and O. J. Simpson was about to be awarded a charter membership until attorney Johnnie Cochran got him off.

Black citizens watch these leaders and see a trend: it's easier to cry racism than to assume any responsibility for your actions. My opinion is: Deal with it, baby, because America doesn't need to keep hearing how oppressed blacks are every time another black public figure gets in trouble. It's like the boy who cried wolf—people stopped coming to his aid, and when he was finally telling the truth, everybody ignored him. We can't cry racism every time something doesn't go our way.

Racism and the Black Politician

Liberal black politicians who have avoided state prison hide behind the same cloak of deception. These elitist whores claim their mission in life is to squelch bigotry, when they are in fact racists themselves. It's not that they hate whites, but they frequently accuse them of hating blacks and judge every issue through race-colored glasses. They are the protectionists of the black cause and every word they utter and every political move they make is predicated on one thing: skin color.

In a public policy forum, if a white male Republican says it's wrong for women to bear children outside of marriage and he no longer wants the government to subsidize this behavior, he is not a fiscal conservative demanding that people start taking responsibility for their actions, he's a racist.

New York Democratic congressman Charles B. Rangel is one of the biggest abusers of this tactic. In legitimate Congressional debates over the cutting of social programs, he leveled this remark at Republicans: "Anytime they talk about lowering taxes and they wear red ties, that's the old KKK." In February 1995, Rangel became furious with the House Ways and Means Committee when it decided to eliminate a tax provision encouraging minority ownership of broadcast properties. Rangel not only accused the committee of scapegoating minorities and immigrants, but compared the committee's tactics to those of Adolf Hitler.

Playing the Race Card

I know all about getting caught after doing something stupid and then playing the race card to avoid suffering the consequences. Folks think O. J. Simpson's lawyers were the first to employ this tactic, but irresponsible people have been doing it for years. Growing up in East St. Louis and Mount Holly, New Jersey, I refused to take any responsibility for the things I did.

My conscience was clear because the popular liberal leaders of the time, along with my high school counselors, drilled into me that from the time blacks are born, they are victims of institutionalized racism. The argument goes that blacks are descendants of slaves and no matter what they learn or how hard they work, whites control their destiny.

The truth is all blacks will experience racism at one time or another in their lives. I'm not excusing bigotry, nor am I advocating that blacks turn their cheeks to discrimination and hatred. However, there's no reason to dwell on it and allow a negative incident to become such a dominating force that you no longer give your fellow man the benefit of the doubt.

Sometimes, when you're digging a foundation and run into a block of granite, it makes more sense simply to go around it and build elsewhere rather than blow up the obstacle and destroy the lot. That's why America is a great place to live today.

White Racism Is a Smoke Screen

I have my own opinion as to why there are so many underachievers in the black community—and I want to add that this is an epidemic plaguing a broad spectrum of Americans, not just blacks and other minorities. I feel we are evolving into a nation of victims, where even our worst conduct can be excused and blamed on someone or something else. Nobody is accountable for his or her own behavior anymore, and part of the reason is that society has been contaminated by the secular humanist victim—"I'm okay and you're okay. Everything is gray and nothing is absolute."

When I was a teenager, that sacrilegious doctrine allowed me to determine right from wrong based on my personal judgments and experiences. Few people close to me had the courage to stand up and tell me that what I was doing was dead wrong. They should have, because I thought I was smarter than everyone else at a time when I didn't have the wisdom to exercise sound judgment. You know, a secularist might even have the audacity to argue that the word *proper* is relative; I know, because I redefined it to fit my lifestyle.

The Nation of Islam and Louis Farrakhan

On the day of the Million Man March back in October 1995, I thought about the Camden, New Jersey, Muslims I had befriended while working at the record store in the summer of 1975. Here was a group that had waited years for its turn on a national stage, and now it was finally happening. The turnout was huge, and it was hailed as a day of celebration and solidarity for black America, even though many blacks object to the Muslim faith.

For me, it was a sad day because I feel the emergence of Farrakhan as a political player has been a step backward for a country that desires to rid itself of racial hatred.

Though voices of moderation were heard at the march, hatemongers like ex–Chicago congressman Gus Savage got his turn on the pulpit. He ignored the march's message of atonement for the sins of the black community and argued that black men have not reacted strongly enough to racism and the "incipient fascism" of white America. The venom was pouring the Friday before the march when a rally of 1,200 black nationalists and fervid Farrakhan supporters gathered in Washington and heard racially inflammatory speeches. "The black holocaust is a hundred times worse than the Jewish holocaust or any other holocaust," said Malik Zulu Shabazz, an organizer of the rally, which was not sanctioned by the Nation of Islam.

Muslim politics are still as vile and spiteful as ever. They are anti-Semitic and believe people with blond hair and blue eyes are devils. Nothing has changed, except that the Nation of Islam's influence over young blacks is more prevalent.

On the day before the march, I appeared on CNN and spoke out about why I could not endorse a rally led by Louis Farrakhan. I said our country should be about unity and Farrakhan has been about divisiveness and separation for many years. Remember, the march took place soon after O. J. Simpson's acquittal, and America desperately needed a healing between the races before the situation spiraled out of control.

Farrakhan's speeches are typically sprinkled with biblical references and themes like atonement. If he were serious about using that word as a rallying cry, then everyone who pranced across the stage at the march should have opened his speech with the words, "I forgive you. Please forgive me." There has been hatred and oppression between all races and Farrakhan blew his chance to extend the olive branch.

There is a successful men's movement in this country that could teach Farrakhan about focus and strategy. It's called Promise Keepers. The membership numbers in the hundreds of thousands and concentrates on racial reconciliation, while the Million Man March was all about Farrakhan's political agenda.

Six months after the Million Man March, I was sitting in a Los Angeles studio getting ready to broadcast my weekday noontime radio show when the Associated Press wire service reported that Farrakhan was soliciting support from Libya's Mu'ammar Gadhafi and Iraq's Saddam Hussein, America's sworn enemies. They were offering Farrakhan big-time pledges—$1 billion from Gadhafi, as it turned out.

That afternoon on my show, the calls started coming in and I raised the issue that if Farrakhan chose to accept donations from terrorists, he should revoke his citizenship and register as a foreign agent. Well, a lot of black callers were not amused by my remarks.

There are aspects of Farrakhan's politics that I support: the moral restraint demonstrated by Muslim men and women, and their emphasis on entrepreneurship and circulating black dollars in the black community. Still, accepting money from an enemy of America is intolerable.

Here's the dilemma blacks will have to face: Do we choose Farrakhan's message of economic empowerment and capitalism, yet with a very violent and separatist overtone, or do we look to the old Democratic socialism as the way to go? I can't help but think there's a third choice: the GOP, which must start appealing to black voters who desperately need an alternative to the Democratic Party. And then maybe in the year 2000 the GOP will be living in the White House, and I'll be invited to stay overnight in Mr. Lincoln's bedroom.

THE BLACK CODE OF SILENCE

I'm so tired of liberal blacks like Al Sharpton and Jesse Jackson belittling conservative black folks as a bunch of callous freaks. When the GOP gained control of Congress after the November 1994 election, Jackson was asked by *The Washington Post* if blacks would benefit by working more closely with the conservative majority. This was Jackson's dismissive response: "The question is working with them on what—going after welfare mothers, dismantling public housing and job training?"

Jackson's mentor, theologian and educator Samuel DeWitt Proctor, took direct aim at black conservatives who were willing to sit down at the bargaining table. "They are either stupidly ahistorical . . . or mendacious parasites who carry the false message that blacks caused their own problems and deserve to suffer."

At the same time, most reasonable blacks who know better refuse to come to our defense. In a 1995 *Washington Post*–ABC News national poll, 46 percent of blacks voiced opposition to affirmative action programs giving preference to minorities, while 52 percent supported them. This is no sweeping endorsement of affirmative action by black voters, but there is no such disagreement in the Congressional Black Caucus. To it, affirmative action is as entrenched as Social Security.

Two years ago, the Reverend Al Sharpton attempted to silence black conservative Supreme Court Justice Clarence Thomas on the affirmative action issue by leading a candlelight vigil with a group of ministers in Fairfax County, Virginia, outside Thomas's home. Sharpton was angry with

Thomas for siding with a majority of the court in putting new restrictions on affirmative action. Sharpton's complaint: Thomas's remark that he "could not embrace racism to deal with racism. It's not Christian."

If you're black, it's taboo to speak out against affirmative action even if you oppose it. Consequently, Thomas has been a whipping boy for black leftists ever since his nomination to the high court. How do they get away with this? The black community has been wimped into a code of silence. Consequently, it has become just another special interest group controlled by liberal Democrats.

Black civil rights leaders know how to keep their sheep in line. Anyone who speaks up is called a racist if he's white and a sellout or a traitor if he's black. That's what Sharpton was insinuating when he scolded minority journalists at their 1994 convention because they had criticized affirmative action. He told them to shut up. "You come in and condemn something that really sponsored your careers," he said, neglecting to add that they don't have a right to change their minds in a free country if they no longer see the value of a gimmee-it-now program.

Conservative Blacks: Breakers of the Code

The civil rights leaders' biggest targets are the black conservatives, who are growing in influence and power. While most blacks unequivocally support their liberal leaders, conservative role models have been ignored, even pilloried by some members of the black community. I'm talking about men like 1996 presidential candidate Alan Keyes and Supreme Court Justice Clarence Thomas. I'm frustrated when I see a list of the top fifty influential blacks in America in *Ebony* magazine's fiftieth-anniversary edition and notice that the number one black publication in the world excluded Judge Thomas from its list. I'm upset but not surprised the editors dismissed him—he is a Republican appointee after all. But I want to know how *Ebony* can include Anita Hill and justify excluding the most influential black in government today? How can they do that and keep a straight face?

Alan Keyes made the rebuilding of the family the primary issue in his presidential bid. There's little doubt that the destruction of the nuclear family is a critical problem, and conservative solutions deserve a look since liberal social programs have not rectified illegitimacy. Yet Keyes was the focus of an article in the October 30, 1995, issue of *The Nation*, in which he was characterized as a "black conservative con artist. Linda Williams, a professor of politics who directs the University of Maryland's Afro-American studies program, ridiculed Keyes as "a fountain of dishonesty and opportunism when he claims that most blacks share his views," although the evidence suggests just the opposite. Williams conceded that "On issues like school prayer, capital punishment, homosexuality, and choice, many blacks have traditionally held conservative views." If she had stopped right there, she would have been accurate in her assessment of the black community.

Liberals, though, don't know when to say enough is enough. Williams went on to argue that blacks don't care about moral issues and family values at the voting booth, noting that fewer blacks voted Republican in 1994 than they did in 1990. I disagree. Blacks do care passionately about conservative issues, only when they go to vote, they stick to the code that they must vote Democratic.

What has happened to the black race? Why have we refused to confront the civil rights establishment and failed to break the code of silence? I know breaking the code can be frightening. I am a female black conservative—a minority within a minority—and it hasn't been easy.

Listen up, folks, the code is destructive and counterproductive. It sucks us down and blinds us from the truth, allowing leaders like the Reverends Jackson and Sharpton and Representative Maxine Waters to fan the flames of institutionalized racism and demand that we unequivocally support all liberal social programs and agendas, regardless of how immoral they are or how badly they've turned out.

Yet within this facade of solidarity, there are fissures and contradictions. As publisher of a Christian magazine that circulated in South Central Los Angeles for nine years, I've met just about every minister in the area. Go to their churches on Sunday and hear their sermons, and you will get a very conservative message emphasizing faith, family, hard work, and moral virtues. But when it comes to publicly defending conservative principles in the community or conservative social policy, they're silent. Why do so many pastors hesitate to criticize liberalism, yet line up like fight fans at Caesar's Palace to rally around the Mike Tysons and O. J. Simpsons of the world? It seems if you suggest that welfare has destroyed black families and serious reform is needed to save our youth, you're committing a bigger crime than rape and wife abuse. Hey friends—criticizing a liberal black leader is not tantamount to spreading a dark family secret.

O. J. Is Guilty—Plain and Simple!

The code of silence was never more apparent in recent times than during the O. J. Simpson murder trial. Let us not forget that the groundswell of emotion that exploded during the Million Man March was fueled by the Simpson verdicts. Like a fault line jarred by an earthquake, the racial divide between blacks and whites that had been tenuously dormant since the 1992 riots split wide open when Simpson walked out of the Los Angeles County jailhouse a free man.

A year earlier, I was guiding a camera crew from a Dutch news agency through South Central Los Angeles. The news agency was preparing a report on the national surveys that showed most whites felt Simpson was guilty and most blacks believed he was innocent. A media acquaintance of mine was working with them, so I agreed to help out and guide them around the city.

Assisted by some of my staffers from the Coalition on Urban Affairs, we interviewed about two hundred blacks. We spoke with folks at a bus stop on the corner of Slauson and Crenshaw; we visited a liquor store at the corner of Florence and Normandie, where truck driver Reginald Denny was nearly beaten to death. Then we drove east and stopped by the offices of the Brotherhood Crusade, where some rap stars were giving out Thanksgiving turkeys.

It was my job to preinterview the subjects, so I asked each person, "Do you think O. J. Simpson's guilty or innocent?" Eighty to ninety percent of the time, the person replied "guilty." Then the television camera would click on, and a white reporter from the Dutch news agency would step up and ask the same question, only the response was completely different. "He's innocent," they said, and many hastened to add, "We'll riot if he's convicted!"

Now I'm hearing all this and I'm thinking, "You're kidding, right?" I just spoke to these people and they changed their answers." So I asked some of them, "Why did you do that? Don't you realize you're sending a message to the nation of Holland that isn't even true?" Some of the responses were, "Who cares," and others were quite defensive—"F— white people." The code was clearly in force on that day.

During the Simpson trial, defense attorney Johnnie Cochran took full advantage of the code of silence. Because of the extent of domestic violence, I initially felt a predominantly female jury might convict Simpson. But when Cochran took special care to inform this panel that they are black first and women second, I felt the jury might let Simpson go. Cochran is not only very persuasive, he holds the kind of power in the black community that could have made some of these jurors feel vulnerable. Whether he would use his influence in such a manner was irrelevant. Those jurors knew he could potentially bring the pressure of the community to bear. Christopher Darden experienced this firsthand when Cochran challenged his ethnicity after Darden argued that Mark Fuhrman's past use of the N word could prejudice the predominantly black jury.

I also believe these jurors felt the burden of their race in other ways. They did not want be called "sellouts" by their neighbors, which explains why so many of the dismissed black jurors said, "Well, the prosecution is making a good case, but . . ." They added that "but" every time. They knew in their hearts Simpson could be guilty, and I believe some may have deliberately wanted off the panel because there were struggling between doing the right thing and convicting him, and going with the flow and letting him go. For these jurors, a vote for conviction would have been tantamount to wearing the scarlet letter back home in their community.

While the code of silence protected Simpson, it nearly destroyed prosecutor Christopher Darden. Why do you think he got so upset with Cochran? Why did Darden lose faith in the judicial system? It was obvious that Cochran was cast as the hero taking on "The Man," and Darden the willing "Tom" collaborating with the enemy. The white legal pundits were calling Darden a token while blacks were labeling him a sellout. Darden was ignored by the black media because he was perceived as a traitor to his race. During the trial, Cochran knew Darden was vulnerable to an attack and that Darden was handcuffed because he would have to take on the lawyer defending a black hero.

Let's face it. There are still flaws in our society that allow blacks to keep a stranglehold on the code of silence. As long as there is bigotry and hatred based on race, large numbers of blacks will feel justified in letting a guilty man walk.

Not that Simpson ever had a great reputation in the black community. On the street, he's a sellout, too. He made it big financially and chose to live in a fancy estate in exclusive Brentwood without giving back a thing. His lifestyle was troubling to many blacks who supported him.

Another mark against Simpson was that he left his black wife for a white woman, and in some circles that makes him worse than dirt. Some black folks would have loved to see him fry, but they can't say it publicly because of the unspoken community pressure to show a unified front.

Blacks also feel resentful over the absurd amount of attention placed on the trial; they felt it had something to do with the defendant, who was black, and the victims, who were white—one of them a beautiful blond woman. Nicole Simpson was not a sympathetic figure in the eyes of many blacks because she must have stolen a black man from his black wife. "She's a slut and it serves her right," was the popular refrain. Hey folks, we can pretend all we want to that we're all politically correct, but even God-fearing people like myself have to fight back those thoughts. There is such a thing as reverse racism.

When it comes to O. J. Simpson, blacks have taken a defensive posture before the white world. They will not concede his guilt even if they know it to be true, and this might explain why all those people who were interviewed by the Dutch reporters changed their answers right before my eyes when confronted on camera by a white questioner. On that day, one year before the acquittal, I drove home believing there was no way a predominantly black jury would convict Simpson.

I knew I was right when jurors who were dropped from the panel had not been persuaded by the state's case against Simpson, even after DNA evidence conclusively showed he was just about the only person on the planet who could have done it. But I was also convinced that those dismissed jurors were lying. They knew he was guilty and so did the final twelve jurors who acquitted him.

It's amazing to me that some of them were actually persuaded by the glove demonstration. Are you kidding? As though Simpson was going to slip that glove on to take his dog for a walk on Rockingham. Then he said in the courtroom, "Oh, it doesn't fit." Yeah right, O. J. C'mon—if you were on trial for murder in front of the whole country, wouldn't you try to pretend that glove was just a teensy-weensy bit small? After that show, it was a done deal.

Simpson is categorically guilty, and the black community knows it. It was easy for me to believe so. The Bible reads that the heart of man is "desperately wicked," so it comes as no shock that a jealous Simpson could have gotten himself in a situation where he lost control with his ex-wife and then turned around to confront her friend.

Have you ever loved someone so much you didn't want to share that person with anyone else? It's no excuse for murder, but people shouldn't be surprised that something like this could happen when it goes on all the time in our society. Simpson may be above the law, but he's still human, and still subject to the same passions and shortcomings as all the rest of us. People get mad at each other all the time, and it's not too difficult to act on anger in a world where there's little restraint. Here was a man who had been coddled, who had acted out every fantasy, and who had gotten away with everything his whole life. It's no wonder he got away with double homicide.

MORAL RESTRAINT

Our schools distribute condoms and teach children that having sex is all right if it's done safely. AIDS, illegitimacy, and drug use are rampant among teens. Could parents get a little tougher on their kids? Can schools start instilling some moral discipline while society gets tougher on its criminals and starts demanding more community involvement in policing neighborhoods? The possible solutions may be closer to home than you think.

The School Condom Debate: My First Foray into Politics

Back in 1991 when my elder daughter was entering junior high, the Los Angeles School Board was debating whether to distribute free condoms to students so they could have safe sex.

Safe sex. My daughter had been in private parochial school and if she had repeated the words *safe sex* in class there, she probably would have felt the sting of a ruler across her knuckles. Life would be much different at *government* school.

You'll notice I said "government" and not "public." I'm not making a mistake. Most public schools these days don't request much parental input and are run by government bureaucrats and the teachers' unions, so I view so-called public schools as a government monopoly that must be broken up. Until that day comes, they remain government schools to me.

The school district was already distributing condoms on a limited basis to students through health clinics in three Los Angeles senior high schools. The district claimed they gave them out only to students who had parental consent.

I had a simple question for the LA School Board. Where did they get off making public health policy when they couldn't even provide my daughter with a locker and some of the books she needed for seventh grade? Where were the priorities?

I joined forces with Reverend Louis Sheldon of the Traditional Values Coalition, whom I had worked with a few years earlier on recruiting black ministers into the coalition. We staged a press conference, and two hundred parents and preachers marched on the school board.

When one of the local Los Angeles radio stations decided to host a debate on condoms in the schools, I volunteered to speak out against the plan. The station had lined up Reverend Cecil Murray to argue in support of the idea. One Sunday, he had given out the AIDS information packets containing the condoms.

I had tried to find a local pastor to debate Reverend Murray, but he's an influential liberal in Los Angeles and nobody wanted to take him on. "I'm not debating him—we will not expose our black brother on white radio even though we don't agree with him," they said. The code of silence was alive once again. It bothered me that men of God were more interested in protecting one of their own than exposing his error. So I volunteered to do the debate.

During the show, Reverend Murray argued that he decided to hand out the condoms because at that time he was burying one person a month who had died from AIDS.

So I said, "Why not teach abstinence? We're talking about a

controllable disease here. If we send out a strong message, we can stop the epidemic." I also suggested that if people want to have sex, they ought to get married. I said handing out condoms is a joke. For most guys, it's like trying to sell the Metro Rail in Los Angeles. People don't want to give up their BMWs.

We've become a fast, convenience-oriented society that prefers drive-through fast-food restaurants and ATM machines to taking a few extra minutes to wait in line. Who's going to take the time to put on a condom? None of the men I had slept with in my promiscuous days ever bothered.

I thought I won the debate but we lost the condom controversy. In 1992, the school board adopted a condom distribution plan and now offers them to all senior high students with parental consent.

Condoms and the AIDS Epidemic

Condoms are by no means a fail-safe method to prevent pregnancy and disease. For influential people to suggest otherwise is not only irresponsible, but dangerous.

The Centers for Disease Control reported that AIDS is the leading cause of death for all people age twenty-five to forty-four. The disease also disproportionately affects black men and women. A recent study showed 1 in 33 black males are infected compared to only 1 in 90 white males. While black and Hispanic women represent 22 percent of the population of all women, they make up 77 percent of all the AIDS cases involving women. And black women alone make up 54 percent of these cases. So clearly, the message to use condoms never got through to them.

Drugs also play a part, and not just the intravenous kind. Folks don't realize they can get AIDS in a pickup bar. People get high, they drink, and then it's, "Who cares, let's go home and have sex."

It's no secret that there's a high rate of homosexual sex in prison. A lot of guys are locked up, come back out, and get back with their girlfriends. One of my old girlfriends had her baby by a former inmate, and I once asked him about the prevalence of prison sex. His response was, "A man's gotta do what a man's gotta do."

That's how it goes. And it keeps going round and round. Yet the best solution liberal policymakers can offer to the AIDS epidemic, and teen sex in general, is to give out condoms. They don't talk about changing attitudes. It's a whole lot easier just to say, "Will somebody get that boy a condom."

There's another reason for the high rate of AIDS in minority areas. It's called the welfare state, a place with a high number of single women heading up households and plenty of roaming men. Yet the government's saying, "Don't be responsible. If you get pregnant, here's a check and here are some food stamps. We're working on a national health plan, so if you abuse your body, we'll take care of you."

AIDS isn't the only reason to challenge irresponsible sex. Today 30 percent of all American children are born out of wedlock and 70 percent of black kids are born without a father in the home. Promiscuous sex is dismantling the tradition of building a marriage before having children.

I'd like to take every single mom out there and the father of her child, grab them by the collar, and ask them, "What do you think daddies are for? They teach their kids how to abstain. They teach their sons about hard work. They teach their daughters to value themselves and their bodies. They tell their girls, 'No, you're not wearing that outfit out of this house. And you *better* be home at eleven o'clock.'"

Many of the social programs aimed at helping single mothers have accomplished only one thing: they've drastically multiplied the number of single mothers. So how about it, parents and teachers? Let's confront these girls and boys and say, "Hold on, you should wait to have sex until you are married." Let's teach those young girls how to reject advances by older men. They might laugh at us for a while, but a Just Say No to Sex campaign might be what this country needs. And perhaps former First Lady Nancy Reagan could lead the way!

You know, trickle-down works. When radical feminists, female pop icons, and the media glorify single motherhood, teenage girls are listening. When male rappers boast about abusing and knocking up their girlfriends, young boys start roaming like dogs in heat.

If single folks would get married, the spread of AIDS and the number of stray kids running around would drop. The number of households headed by single women would decrease dramatically and promiscuity and illegitimate births would diminish. So I repeat, no more subsidies for stupid behavior!

Sex Before Marriage: A Little Shame Goes a Very Long Way

First the Los Angeles Unified School District started giving out condoms. Now guess what they have on their hands: scores of teen mothers. So what's the solution to the problem? Of course, create yet another program.

In case you haven't heard, the district operates day-care centers in high schools for teen mothers. The thinking goes that the girls will profit because now they can stay in school without having to worry about child care. That's not only wasteful, but once again, we have another government entity playing parent. Families, not schools, should be kicking in to help a young mother.

If a fifteen-year-old girl decides to get pregnant out of wedlock, I don't think the errant behavior should be rewarded with membership in the teen mommies club at the local high school. What's to discourage this girl from getting pregnant again? Even more critical, what's there to dampen the enthusiasm of a female classmate who might be feeling left out of the mix? Life should be hard because these young mothers need to realize they should be married before they have another baby.

As usual, the lewd left claims this social program is intended to *help* these disadvantaged girls. Do they stop to think such programs might promote rather than hinder the problem behavior—having sex and getting pregnant in the first place? As a society, we've got to send tougher messages to our young people. I sure don't feel comfortable with my daughter sitting next to a pregnant classmate in geometry class.

There's another alternative, by the way, to handing over some condoms and birth control pills to keep your daughter from getting pregnant. First, try some one-on-one discussions. I've had long talks about sex with my oldest girl, Angel. She's been boy-crazy for a couple of years now and that's okay. Yet I insist she understand the value of sexual purity and the sanctity of saving herself for her wedding night.

I'm sure she's going to be challenged, and society is not making it any easier for her. Our church has been the only place that has reinforced this important message. I believe she will wait, though she does threaten to get married from time to time. Ha! We'll see about that.

Hey, Hillary! You Listening?

At the rate our government schools are going, they'll be holding teen wedding ceremonies during recess if we're not careful. The government sure knows how to pile on the programs. Do you think it ever occurred to education policy-makers that the reason we now have teen day care is because we started teaching sex education in the first place? I don't think this thought occurred to First Lady Hillary Rodham Clinton, author of *It Takes a Village*. Sorry Hillary—school is no substitute for a child's family. According to African tradition, the village you mention in your book refers to private citizens tending to the needs of neighbors. Sort of like being our brother's keeper. Like all good government social-ists, the First Lady has stretched the concept "It takes a village to raise a child" to mean that government can usurp authority over parents.

Sex education is a fine example of school bureaucrats deciding they can do a better job than parents when it comes to teaching children about intimacy. It is virtually mandatory in school curriculums nationwide. Of course, since the intro-duction of sex education, more kids are doing it today than ever before. And we thought kids weren't listening in class.

One night over dinner, I got into a conversation with my daughter over sex education. In health class, I explained, you're taught about the four basic food groups, but no secularist school bureaucrat will ever come into my home and tell me what to feed my family because it's good for them. Still, schools do tell young people how to have sex, and will even provide them with condoms, if necessary. This is defi-nitely an intrusion on a family's privacy.

The problem with sex education is that it goes way beyond

explaining the intricacies of the human body, such as menstruation and human reproduction. In *The Atlantic Monthly* author Barbara Whitehead wrote that comprehensive sex education "sweeps across disciplines, taking up the psychology of relationships, sociology of the family and the sexology of masturbation and massage."

Yet for all the talk about safe sex and condoms, the National Center for Health Statistics provides some disconcerting news: three of every four disadvantaged teens still don't use condoms, and consequently our country is absorbing more than 1 million teen pregnancies a year. Of these, about 400,000 abort, 100,000 miscarry, and nearly 500,000 children are carried to term. About two-thirds of these children are born to unmarried girls. So kids in school are learning how to do it but only taking part of the lesson with them. I don't call that effective education.

Say a Little Prayer

There's another thing schools can do to instill some moral restraint in their students: Start each day with a prayer.

I don't see why lewd leftists are so adamant about keeping prayer out of government schools. I favor a few moments of silence at the start of each school day because it'll let kids know that there are boundaries to their behavior and there is a higher authority who can exercise judgment over them. That's right, prayer instills a little fear and I don't think that's such a bad thing.

Many children lack a sense of humility and don't respect authority. Prayer helps establish that basis for respect, not only for God, but for all types of authority figures—ranging from parents to teachers to police officers.

During this moment of silence, we are acknowledging that something out there is bigger than us, and if you don't answer to it here you just may have to elsewhere. I'm not saying school children must pray to God during this private time, but at the very least a moment of silence helps a teacher set some ground rules at the start of the day, which can't hurt. So bow your head and close your eyes, kids, you could all use a little old-fashioned discipline.

The Drug Catastrophe

One of the consequences of lax discipline and the absence of moral restraint is the rise in drug use. Once again, it's making headlines as a huge problem among teenagers, partly because their parents also used and now feel they don't have the authority to warn their kids of the dangers. That kind of tolerance is unacceptable.

The lewd left often dismisses religion as having nothing beneficial to offer society, but I'll tell you this, it could help young people from getting mixed up with drugs. You know my story: God helped me get off drugs once and for all.

I feel narcotic use among teenagers is out of control because families are losing their faith in a higher authority. In fact, too many young people may not even know one exists unless their parents take them to church. Lord knows they won't learn about God in a government school.

I put drug use down as a last resort to coping with guilt. Some folks pray to God, others talk to a psychologist, have anonymous sex, or work it off in a gym. Others turn to alcohol and drugs to escape. When I used angel dust, I had no moral code to show me when I did something wrong, so I used it again and again, and it made me feel better until I came back down from my high.

People also feel the need to flee from reality because there is no escape from the truth. By that I mean just because lewd leftists tend to excuse people's rebellious behavior because of their upbringing or lousy environment, the troublemakers still know they've done something wrong even if they have only half a conscience. Why not put your trust in a Lord who can forgive you for sinning? Where else can you find that kind of release?

Drug Dealers—Mow My Lawn!

I know one thing—we've got to close our borders to drug runners and make certain the penalties for these crimes are as severe as for aiming a missile at our country. At the same time, I have a problem with filling prisons with drug dealers and users as a method of dealing with this insufferable virus that's infecting our inner cities. That's only getting us closer to a police state. We need to attack the root cause of drug use—the demand. We will make no inroads in curbing demand until we take steps toward developing moral fiber in our young people.

In the meantime, something needs to be done. I would like to see a little retribution to the families who are victimized by drug dealers. I'd certainly want some retribution if some kid ever sold drugs to one of my daughters. I'd want that person paying me back directly—and if he or his family doesn't have the money, that individual should have to work for me, not get sent off to some juvenile detention center on my dime where he gets three squares a day and a roof over his head for a few months before he's let out on the street to do it all over again!

In August 1996, I appeared on the Comedy Central channel's *Politically Incorrect* show and I made the argument that slavery as an institution isn't wrong, and it has been distorted by the lewd left. The world has always had slaves and America actually inherited the practice from Great Britain. Indentured servants, for example, earned their freedom after working seven years.

The problem was how America implemented slavery, basing it on race instead of the character of the person. Enslaving black Americans was a crime against humanity, but I don't have a problem with a prison inmate paying restitution to his victim. That's not slavery, that's justice!

Street Monitors

Ever have something stolen from your home, and then suffer the indignity of having the investigating police officer ask you how to spell the name of the street you live on? If a police officer doesn't live in your community or know his way around the 'hood, how will he ever catch anyone committing a crime there? A strategy that encourages local participation in policing and rewards officers who know the turf could cut into crime dramatically.

Neighborhoods need to monitor their own residents. Private security and local police precincts, in partnership with homeowners and tenants, can get the job done without answering to a massive central administration. The contributions from citizens would range from volunteering at local stations to turning in criminals they know are terrorizing their neighborhoods. This won't happen if law enforcement is viewed as the enemy, which is how much of the black community perceives them. It's gotten so bad that it's getting harder for young blacks to consider serving as police officers because they don't want to be labeled sellouts.

The Death Penalty

One of government's few roles in society should be making its citizens feel safe and secure. The death penalty is the ultimate form of authority for the civil government to use in maintaining control. I support it for three crimes—murder, rape, and kidnapping. It's needed for murder because there is no other form of retribution for taking another life; it's necessary for rape because what a rapist steals from a person can never be recovered. And I endorse it for kidnapping because when you put a person's life in danger, that individual will never feel secure again.

The lewd left says we shouldn't be so harsh on our criminals, particularly since we can't dispense equitable justice. That means rich defendants can hire a good lawyer to get them off while the poor are defenseless, and therefore they deserve the benefit of the doubt.

Sorry, it doesn't matter if a murderer is destitute—he deserves to be judged. We have plenty of appeals and checks in place to make sure wrongly accused people aren't put to death, but just because one innocent person may die for every hundred who are guilty, that's no reason to ban the death penalty. How many murders do we have to read about before we get serious? Unless we avenge hideous crimes, criminals will have no fear and we will never be safe.

PART 3

Weaning Us off Government Dependency

Americans don't need bureaucrats running their lives. They should have the freedom to send their children to any school they want; they shouldn't have to be dependent on a bi-monthly welfare check to survive when there's probably a business around the corner from their home that could pay them a decent wage. That will take a little help from an imaginative government and strong conservative leaders from all races.

MY DREAM FOR OUR SCHOOLS

When I was growing up, I slid right through the government schools I attended in East St. Louis, Illinois, and Mount Holly, New Jersey. I passed without cracking a book, and that should tell you plenty about the state of our government-run schools. They are in dire need of an overhaul—just like my old Peugeot.

I kept that car running long after it had outlived its usefulness, but that's no way to treat our education system. Today, kids are inundated with stuff from television and the media, and it frustrates me that government schools provide no moral lessons since religion has been purged from curriculums nationwide.

Take our government schools in Los Angeles. They are so plagued by high dropout rates (44 percent), gang crime, unmotivated teachers, and bored students that even the mayor agrees we should break up the massive district of 650 schools.

Another thing about these schools: They fail to recognize that parents don't want their kids treated as guinea pigs in the education system's attempt to solve the social ills of the world. At the very least, we want our children to have the ability to read and write to go along with that diploma, and our expectations are much higher than that. Schools need to help kids identify their talents so they can develop a work ethic. We're talking about providing survival skills.

Let me tell you about my dream for educating the children of this country. I envision neighborhoods filled with private schools on every street corner. They would be driven by the free market system—the same one that provides us with some of the best consumer products in the world. We could create schools specializing in entrepreneurship, crafts, engineering, computers, college prep, and other trades. Each one would teach reading, writing, and math, but the rest of the curriculum would be dedicated to job training or education in a field determined by free-market forces. It's not so far-fetched—in Los Angeles we already have public specialty schools in our district's magnet programs that focus on academic specialties, but only a certain number of students can get in. So what about everyone else? And what about the kids who aren't college material?

We could pay for private school tuition with school choice scholarships by drawing from the tax dollars now set aside for public education. Then there would be nothing to stop a great teacher from saying, "Hey, I know twenty-five people who need this type of school, and I could start it." I look around South Central and notice there are nail shops and liquor stores on most every corner. Why not a school on every corner?

School choice scholarships would give poor inner-city kids a chance at a future. Right now, states set aside money from property taxes to fund schools. In California, it works out to be around $5,200 per student. I believe each family with school-age children should have a voucher for at least half that amount for use at a government, private, or parochial school.

I don't see this as draining money from government schools, I see it as forcing them to compete. It will make them better and more accountable to the community they serve. If they have to compete for dollars, they will cut out the fat and spend the money where it needs to be spent—just like any other business.

One Final Word on Vouchers

Former Republican presidential candidate Bob Dole promised he would work to develop a voucher program providing American families up to $1,500 per student to enroll them in the school of their choice. He didn't have to look far to find a pilot program since two states—Wisconsin and Ohio—have already installed voucher programs for low-income inner-city residents. A California ballot initiative that would have given parents a $2,600 voucher for each child for use at private schools failed to pass in 1992.

But in both Wisconsin and Ohio, surveys show low-income children using vouchers are reaping the rewards of higher test scores and safer environments. Kids are actually looking forward to going to school in those communities, and why not? Ironically, our most vocal opponents to school choice— Democrats like President Clinton, Vice President Gore, and Jesse Jackson—sent their children to private schools. They're among the privileged few who can afford to choose between a private and public education. All I'm asking is the same courtesy to be extended to low-income Americans, who are a little tired of being slaves to the impersonal government education machine.

The Case for a Private Sectarian Education

This year, my daughter Angel will graduate from a government high school, but I firmly believe her academic success can be attributed to having attended a private religious school in South Central Los Angeles during the first six years of her education. The key components were discipline, moral instruction, and a no-nonsense curriculum emphasizing the basics. She wore a uniform, went to chapel, and if somebody in her class acted up, teachers and principals were permitted to spank.

Do you all remember Damian Williams? He was the guy standing over Reginald Denny's head with a brick in his hand. Well, Damian's mother lived a few blocks from the school my oldest daughter attended—the Frederick K. C. Price III Elementary and Junior High School.

The government school in Damian's neighborhood was a place where many kids didn't go to class and teachers were afraid to enforce the rules or didn't care. When I saw Damian's mother on TV during her son's trial in 1993, she was always crying and talking about Jesus. She obviously had trouble raising her boy and I believe had we been able to give that woman a voucher for $2,600.00—half of what it costs to put a child through California public school—we might have have been able to save her son, who wound up a school dropout.

When Damian was a little boy hanging out with the wrong crowd, she could have ushered Damian to a local private school, begged the headmaster to do whatever it took to control him, and been able to pay that school's tuition with a voucher. If Damian had ended up in the headmaster's office and been on the receiving end of a big stick, that probably would have been fine by Mrs. Williams. The last thing she wanted was for her son to end up in prison.

Now look at him. We are paying $26,000.00 a year to house this young man in state prison. There's something wrong with this picture. If we got the private sector involved in education, an entrepreneur might just open a school for people like Damian Williams who need a little bit of guidance in their early years to get off on the right foot. They may not have to learn Latin or European History, but you know what?

They're going to learn the basics and get the tools they need to succeed in life.

Parochial Schools: A Lesson for Instilling Morality

In South Central Los Angeles and other black neighborhoods, I envision a major role for church-based schools. Morally based education already serves a major portion of this country and there are parents like myself who applaud the complementary value of religious training.

It doesn't matter whether the school is Catholic, or another Christian denomination, Muslim or Jewish—the church is the number one institution in the black community to fight social problems. This is the place where young men can get exposure to positive male role models on a daily basis and develop self-esteem. The critics always claim, "No, no, we must have separation of church and state," and therefore no tax dollars can be spent on these schools. But by excluding church schools from the voucher equation, you are condemning many children to certain failure.

Strippers

There's another thing government schools are failing miserably at: preparing kids for finding work after graduation. When I speak at high school career days, I sometimes start off by saying, "How many of you know what a stripper is?" The kids start laughing. It reminds me of the time I told some folks back home in New Jersey that I was studying marketing and they thought I was going to go to work for a grocery store—stock girl, no doubt.

Then I tell these kids that in the printing business, stripping is an entire trade and those guys are starting at thirty bucks an hour. Suddenly, the laughing stops and their mouths are hanging open. All during my career as a magazine publisher, I tell them, I never saw a black in one of these stripping jobs. So why are there few blacks in this business? I realized the main reason was there were certain industries blacks knew nothing about. One of the reasons why is our educational system.

Our current teaching formula spends little time identifying and cultivating individual talents that can lead to careers or even additional education. Growing up, I went through the motions in school. Few teachers paid any attention to me and I didn't pay any attention to them. My talent—the ability to gab—either went unnoticed or got me into trouble. Yet it was that talent that helped me succeed later in life in sales, radio, television, and motivational speaking.

What our government education system is good at is hustling everyone into one big room and trying to teach them all the same things. Then we wonder why some kids lose interest. Well, if you're interested in fixing cars or painting pictures, you're going to be bored by algebra and French. When you get right down to it, does every kid going through public school need to know a foreign language or chemistry? I feel whether kids are interested in cars or computers, we need to find out those talents early so we can keep their interest in education and prepare them for life beyond school.

MEANINGFUL WELFARE REFORM

On March 24, 1995, the House of Representatives passed a welfare reform bill in an attempt to put an end to the madness. The legislation proposed getting the federal government out of the welfare business and giving control back to the states in the form of block grants. On that day, I spent the morning lobbying conservative Democrats on Capitol Hill to support the bill and later that day had the honor of checking off the Personal Responsibility Act box on the GOP's Contract With America.

At a press conference, I joined with several welfare reform champions, including Congressmen Dick Armey, Jim Talent, and Clay Shaw, and Wisconsin governor Tommy Thompson. I told the media what I liked about the reforms: that they gave families, communities, and churches the privilege of caring for the poor without competition from the federal government.

But this doesn't go far enough. Our current welfare system should be completely abolished and rebuilt from the ground up, just like a building with a ruined foundation. You don't keep building on top of that concrete slab, you tear it down and start over.

There are some very practical things that have to be done. Families have to take a greater role in caring for their own and not relying on taxpayers. Our budget deficit keeps mounting and if somebody doesn't make some sacrifices now, our children and their children will suffer. It just may mean that black Americans will have to bear the burden of caring for our own. When I went off the county, I relied on friends and family until I could find a job, and this is what it's going to take on a much larger scale.

In the long run, finding some kind of job is better than receiving a welfare check that dwindles due to cutbacks and inflation. Let me explain. In 1995, I published an article in *Policy Review* that compared the benefits received by a welfare family to the income earned by a working family. The household consisted of a thirty-eight-year-old grandmother living in Los Angeles with her sixteen- and eighteen-year-old daughters, both of whom have children, receive AFDC, food stamps, Section 8 rent credit, and HMO medical services.

Their combined monthly government package was equivalent to about $2,135.

Now consider what their lives would be like without government assistance: Both teenagers find minimum-wage jobs bringing in $700 a month each, while their mother baby-sits their three children for free and takes in three more at $50 per child per week, or over $600 a month. If the men who fathered these children contributed even as little as $100 per child a month, this household would have another $300 a month. Add it all up, and the combined income is $2,300 a month, less taxes.

Not only does the working family make more, dispelling any notion that minimum-wage earners cannot survive, imagine how much better off that family could be five years from now when those girls are earning higher salaries? Maybe even one of them will be on her way toward earning a college degree.

So for some folks, it might mean moving back in with mom to make ends meet. The liberals want us to think that everyone lives in a victimized home and is being abused, or that parents are too selfish to take back their kids. That's only a small percentage, and those recipients can be helped through shelters and group homes if necessary.

Most people on welfare I talk to have middle-class family members who could provide some kind of help if welfare wasn't there. Sure it would be inconvenient and a hardship, but isn't that what families are for in times of crisis?

Blacks today make up more than one-third of the AFDC roll. It's a disgrace. While we have a growing middle class, we also have more than 1.8 million black families on public assistance. That's shameful. What do we need to do to get welfare families back in the mix?

Besides getting help from relatives, the key will be the ability of community-based organizations and institutions to provide welfare moms job assistance, etiquette skills, education, and lessons in moral responsibility.

It certainly doesn't mean leaving women and children starving on the streets. The House version of the welfare reform bill called for eliminating aid to unwed minor mothers and capping benefits at one child, though the Senate eventually rejected the latter provision. The House also voted that welfare recipients must work after two years with a full cutoff after five years, which was eventually adopted into law.

The legislation is a huge step forward, but to encourage mobility up the economic ladder for single mothers, the government should offer incentives to community-based groups and businesses to become more involved. This is one business that needs a middle man—the government should not be issuing checks directly to consumers.

However, I don't favor proposals to abandon young mothers. We need sensible programs that will teach these women the self-reliance skills and work ethic needed to survive on their own.

With that in mind, I developed a model program based on my own experiences as a welfare mom, an employer of welfare mothers, and an entrepreneur who had difficulty getting started because labor costs were so prohibitive. It's a model that attempts to bring together two struggling elements of black communities: small businesses and a glut of under-skilled welfare mothers. It also capitalizes on one of our strengths: churches.

In this program, there's a project director who recruits thirty small urban businesses that are in need of employees but can't hire them because they can't afford the cost. These businesses are then matched with thirty welfare mothers age sixteen to twenty-five who need a job. In addition, ten churches are approached to provide day care for three children each and several volunteers are recruited to drive the mothers to and from work if transportation is unavailable.

The women may live on their own, in a structured group home setting with other single mothers, or preferably with a mentor family that receives a tax credit for opening its home to a welfare mom. This is one way government can help if it insists on being involved in the social service business: by providing tax breaks to families working with the moms.

Church day care must be part of the solution, even if it means using government-provided vouchers to support the child-care services. In black neighborhoods, churches have the best track record for helping people, and they have the foundation to instill some moral training in the mothers and children involved. Why should we support only nonsectarian child-care providers who teach their participants nothing about right from wrong?

Employers also bear a huge responsibility; they're the ones who must train the welfare mothers so they can later join that company or move on to another job. The business is also the entity that receives the welfare check, which it pays the recipient after she has completed the work requirements.

The good part of the deal is that the business owner gets an employee at low cost and taxpayers get a welfare mom well on her way toward getting off the county.

People think I'm harsh when I say let's get rid of welfare. But it's time for the federal government to put up a sign that reads, "Sweetheart, we are closed and out of the social services business. No new applicants need apply."

WHAT'S SO WRONG WITH CAPITALISM?

Like any entrepreneur, when I started up my magazine my goal was to make a profit. I took my revenue and reinvested it in the business, which allowed me to hire more staff and improve the quality of my product. My opinion on entrepreneurship is that people with clever ideas deserve to be financially rewarded. In return, they keep our economy going strong.

The lewd left often takes a different view toward business owners. They say they are not to be trusted. Owners are tyrants-in-waiting bent on exploiting the working class. Without excessive government regulation, the lewd left insists that capitalists will underpay workers, poison our air and water, and destroy animal and sea life. So the powerful environmental and labor union groups constantly lobby the federal government to check business growth. In California, there is so much overregulation that companies are moving out and not being replaced by start-up ventures or established businesses from other states. Not surprisingly, our inner cities have suffered the worst.

Redlining vs. Self-help

In 1994, I attended a crime summit in Washington, D.C., hosted by the Rainbow Coalition. During one panel discussion, the late Dr. Tom Skinner, a minister and urban consultant from Baltimore, Maryland, confronted Jesse Jackson, who was arguing that racism was preventing young blacks from obtaining work.

In his presentation, Dr. Skinner countered that unemployment could be attributed to the suppression of the entrepreneurial spirit in the inner city. Quoting statistics gathered by the Small Business Administration, he said that small businesses were the number one creators of new jobs in urban areas. Dr. Skinner wasn't about to cry racism as an excuse. He stressed that blacks were partly to blame because they don't spend money in their own neighborhoods. He said if blacks would circulate 25 percent of their dollars locally instead of spending them outside the community, three million new jobs would be created in those communities.

This spending philosophy is one thing Louis Farrakhan and I agree on. I am all for blacks circulating their money in their neighborhoods, banking at community banks, and attending all-black schools. When Dr. Skinner was finished, Reverend Jackson immediately dismissed him: Don't start talking about that self-help our enemies talk about, he said.

Then the other panelists—in the usual lewd lockstep—started agreeing with Jackson. They concluded that it was more important to stop major banks from redlining areas than urging blacks to infuse struggling community banks with sorely needed deposits.

I don't mean to dismiss redlining. Numerous laws have been passed to end it, but guess what? Many banks ignore the laws and keep on redlining. Clearly, going to court isn't about to change the plight of our urban neighborhoods, and frankly, I'm sick and tired of attempts by our civil rights leaders to level the so-called playing field to the detriment of other solutions.

Blacks should focus their efforts on creating our own means of financing, which includes depositing our money in banks that reinvest in black neighborhoods. Not only may the redlining banks change their discriminatory patterns, but neighborhood banks will have the assets to invest in the areas they serve, much as Asian banks support their community of people. Increased competition, not feeble antiredlining legislation, is the answer to changing discriminatory loaning practices.

It could take a while for community banks to fill the void. The black middle class might have to make a sacrifice now so later generations can thrive. It might mean getting slightly less interest on deposits and paying higher interest rates on loans—but in the long run, it's the best way to finance ventures in poor neighborhoods.

Abolish the Minimum Wage

One of the biggest obstacles to inner-city employment is the minimum wage. Democrats are always fighting to increase the minimum wage, but obviously very few have ever owned a small business. If they did, they'd understand how difficult it is to pay an unskilled seventeen-year-old $4.75 an hour, not to mention the training costs and overhead required to maintain low-wage, high-turnover positions.

I ask you, how much do you need to pay someone who sweeps the floor part-time? Folks have no business wanting to sweep all their lives. They should learn to dress windows so they can make $3 an hour. They should learn to cashier to make $4 an hour. If they can do them all, maybe they deserve $10 an hour. If they're smart, they'll get educated and learn how to run that business so they can make even bigger money.

But the lewd left insists that if the minimum wage is abolished, greedy corporations will automatically cut pay to minimum-wage workers. Some liberals obviously have no confidence in the current market system in which competition requires major companies to pay quality employees well. Today, even nominal jobs have such high turnover costs that it's often more expedient for employers to pay a fair wage than risk losing that employee. Simply put, it doesn't pay to be cheap.

The lewd left, however, believes the American economy is permanently rooted in the industrial age. What they forget is that the work force is much more educated and sophisticated when it comes to negotiating wages and working conditions. Today, the employee actually serves as a "moral compass" for the employer.

Blue-collar workers, however, persist in believing they need a union working on their behalf. Face it: Unions are dying because advances during the industrial age have enabled workers to become viable consumers with the highest standard of living in the world. So not only does the worker assemble the various products, he purchases them, doubling his value to the employer. Corporations also have learned something from decades of labor strife—that rewarding productivity fairly reduces turnover and strengthens the product, leading to greater profits.

All that increasing the minimum wage accomplishes is reducing the number of entry-level positions an employer can offer—hence the high unemployment rates in inner cities, where there are few jobs to go around in the first place. However, at slightly lower wages and breaks on taxes for disability and Social Security, a business could hire two people for the price of a little more than one. Production would increase and the business could expand, leading to more jobs.

Hiking the minimum wage creates another problem: government, not labor, determining the worth of particular jobs. Consider domestic labor in Southern California. Most Californians would be happy to pay their illegal help $20 for cleaning a 2,000-square-foot home, but the laborers won't allow it. Without a union, they command $50 and up for the job. But when the government determines worth, as with minimum-wage jobs, willing workers cannot sell their labor at a price that's acceptable to them. So in the end, unskilled and minority workers are hurt most by these laws.

Minimum wage also infringes on job mobility. Changing jobs is a natural growth process for people on the bottom rung of the employment ladder. As you move up, another spot is created for an entry-level worker. But if the salary for entry-level workers is so high it hurts their motivation to advance, there is no movement. It's like being in school. If you don't graduate, there are no seats for the incoming class. The work force becomes stagnant.

A Plan for the Inner City

"We don't have access to capital," is the common refrain I hear from fellow black entrepreneurs. Yet if they understood how the capital gains tax restrains investors from putting their savings at risk, affecting the availability of venture capital, they'd be more open to Republican efforts to abolish the tax. I support the bill of Congressmen Jim Talent and J. C. Watts entitled the Personal Economic Empowerment Act of 1996. This bill would create one hundred "Renewal Communities"—areas with a poverty rate greater than 20 percent and unemployment rates one and a half times the national average. In these zones, capital gains taxes would be eliminated on investments in stock, business property, or partnerships within the zone if those assets are held for five years or longer. The bill also includes tax credits for commercial revitalization and for hiring disadvantaged workers—including welfare mothers and other general relief recipients who need to fulfill work requirements or may be nearing the end of their welfare time limit.

This is the type of legislation that will allow the private sector to create jobs in disadvantaged neighborhoods and enable people on welfare to get off assistance by finding work close to home. In 1997, I'll be working very hard on the House and Senate floors to see that the Personal Economic Empowerment Act is passed into law.

STAR'S GUIDE TO THE PLAYERS

Republicans I Love
JACK KEMP

Now this man is the model for conservatism meeting compassion—and *exactly* the kind of conservative I want to be. When I debate liberals, they often accuse me of bashing welfare because it's in vogue. Sorry, but I've been attacking welfare for years because I'm disgusted with the way it has contributed to lawlessness and the destruction of black families.

I realize change won't happen overnight. We can't uproot programs and policies that have been in place for decades without taking care of the people caught in the stampede. There have to be transition programs in place, which is what I like about Mr. Kemp. He isn't just interested in scaling the highest peak; he wants to make sure he's prepared to get back down.

This has gotten him into some trouble with fellow Republicans. After he was nominated as Mr. Dole's running mate, he caught a lot of flak for criticizing California Proposition 187—a 1995 ballot initiative that passed overwhelmingly and would deny social services to illegal immigrants. His complaint was similar to mine: What do you with a kid who has lived in the United States all his life because his parents illegally immigrated? That child may not even speak a sentence of his native language, let alone survive in his parents' native country, so how can you deport him? Or toss him out of school? Proposition 187 didn't address that issue, so I can't fault Mr. Kemp's position, as much as I don't support subsidies for illegal immigrants.

PAT BUCHANAN

Pat is great for the Republican Party because he serves as a personal reminder of the character and principles we truly stand for. If the GOP is the standard bearer for moral conservatism, he is one of the leaders we have been able to count on election after election. (Perhaps even in the next election.) Right now the Republican Party is at the center of a bitter internal fight between moral conservatives and libertarians, with the moderates stuck in the middle.

The primary issue dividing the sides is abortion, which has been grinding away at the party like a nest of termites in a woodpile. Since 1992, when Dan Quayle's Murphy Brown speech brought family values to the forefront, abortion seized the attention of the GOP. The focus on family values quickly shifted into an abortion debate, pitting the moderate and libertarian factions against the religious right.

This election year was no different. Senator Dole represented the moderate portion of the party while Steve Forbes was trumpeted by the libertarians. Pat Buchanan won the support of the moral conservatives, and he was the only man among the three who was willing to bring the concerns of the unborn before the voters of America.

Buchanan's contribution has added strength to the GOP because the influx of moral conservatives is the only real growth the Republican Party has experienced over the last decade. Motivated by their religious faith, these voters were the group largely responsible for the GOP regaining control of Congress in 1994 and again in 1996.

NEWT GINGRICH

The Contract with America was brilliant, and Newt did a terrific job leading America into the Republican revolution. But after he got blindsided by the liberal media and Democrats using scare tactics about little old ladies and poor children dying in the streets, he backed off. Newt reacted by focusing on image and politics rather than the future of America, and I'm disappointed he didn't have enough confidence in voters who knew he was right.

Children don't like discipline, but they need it so they can learn to make proper choices. Parents know when to stand up to their kids, and when some voters cried, "No fair!" Mr. Gingrich should have confronted these naysayers even if it meant getting dumped out of office in the next election. He was like a doctor who refused to give a child a shot because the baby was throwing a tantrum.

He should have stood his ground on most of his proposals, including Medicare reform and dismantling the Department of Education. I don't think he's aware of just how many people would like to see changes in the Social Security system. The lewd left likes to call him an "extremist," but Newt, extreme is what we need if we're ever going to knock down this budget deficit and reduce taxes.

ALAN KEYES

It's too bad the nation was not ready for Alan Keyes to become the first black president of America, passing him over for their dreams of Colin Powell. With his passion and demand that we stand for truth, Keyes could lead us toward claiming our moral destiny. His credentials are outstanding—a doctorate from the Harvard School of Government and the former ambassador to the United Nations Economic and Social Council. Still, the old guard Republicans ignore him because he speaks out against immorality, racism, and corruption. Let's face it, folks, wherever there's money and power, those three evils aren't far behind. And Alan won't hesitate to shine the light on darkness—no matter who's under the covers.

J. C. WATTS

This Oklahoma congressman's star is rising so fast that someday Nike may even give him his own athletic shoe line. But most important to me, J.C. is a rising star in the minds of young black men and women. He came up from poverty, excelled as a football player and as a preacher, and made it all the way to Capitol Hill. He's proof America can work for blacks and that racism does not stand in the way of achievement.

Republicans Who Should Have Done Better

COLIN POWELL

He is a war hero with leadership potential. While brilliant and successful, he doesn't have a clue about how a social issue like abortion affects our stability as a nation. A military strategist like Powell should be carefully monitoring how abortion is corrupting our collective soul. Meanwhile, many members of the Republican Party are abandoning the moral high ground and rallying around Powell because the color of his skin lends credibility to the GOP. But by embracing an abortion advocate, these Republicans are ignoring one of the causes of our country's moral decline.

BOB DOLE

He's a principled man who should have taken the moral high road during his campaign for president. He was counseled to play up the economic issues, like lowering taxes, when he was the lone candidate who could have served as a referendum on the baby boom generation and what has gone wrong with America in the past thirty years.

He should have spelled out exactly what happened—that his generation fought a war for Democracy and the next generation bought into government dependency. He needed to rally those baby boomers who have begun adopting values they once shunned, such as religion, fiscal responsibility, and moral integrity.

During the Republican primaries, conservative newspaper columnist Cal Thomas urged Dole to capitalize on a powerful message: America needs to return to the time-honored virtues of the post–World War II generation, when young people were willing to die for their country and families could achieve the American Dream with only one parent working.

Bill Clinton can't represent these values. As Mr. Thomas wrote, Clinton came from a generation of sixties radicals who destroyed many of the ideals that made this country great and plunged urban America into an economic and spiritual malaise. Clinton's refusal to endorse most of the Contract With America is evidence that he is a pretender to the so-called moderate Democratic throne. Mr. Dole, a product of the Great Depression and a veteran of World War II, could have persuaded Americans to look within ourselves for solutions, and not be so dependent on government. He could have stood for something greater than all the gimmee-it-now programs combined: faith and self-sufficiency, not dependency on entitlements.

This is the kind of leadership we'll need if we can ever hope to reverse the crumbling of the family and the moral decay that reek havoc in poor neighborhoods.

Democrats We Can Do Without

BILL CLINTON, KING PIMP

This man is a crafty secular socialist. He wants to take care of everyone's tuition bills for college and pay for everybody's medical bills even if it means bankrupting the country. He has done a cunning job playing to the selfish motives of voters who don't want to give anything up.

Pushy, arrogant, and manipulative, he exhibits all the finest qualities of the elite baby boomers. He keeps women secure in the knowledge they don't need men to survive and what they can't provide for themselves, government will. He's a Big Daddy pimp promising to take care of all his whores and welfare brats as long as they keep sending half their paycheck to Washington.

And what a daddy he is. Here is a man with a long history of not being able to govern his private affairs in charge of governing our country. We've bought into the lie that we can't judge someone else's behavior; we have let down our moral guard so far that now anything goes. What else was campaign strategist Dick Morris, a married man who got caught with a prostitute, other than a reflection of the man he was working for? Tell me, would you want a certified public accountant running your business if you found out he was being investigated for tax fraud? I want to know—how can an adulterer be faithful to his own country if he can't be faithful to his own wife?

Clinton is popular because he is a reflection of the baby boom generation that got us into all this trouble. But a vote for Dole was tougher because it was like finally agreeing with your parents after bad-mouthing them all these years. That wasn't about to happen for most baby boomers. Bill's our buddy and our homey, and you don't vote against a homey.

HILLARY CLINTON, QUEEN PIMP

As a first lady, she's done a lousy job. Do you find it odd that the same people who would frown on a wife telling her husband how to run the company he's in charge of have no qualms about Mrs. Clinton lending a hand in the day-to-day affairs of running the United States? She may be a lawyer, but she's no elected official and has no business consulting on a national health plan, in which she got in way over her head.

My question for Mrs. Clinton is this: When you consider the number of broken homes in America and the number of moms working at the expense of raising their children, couldn't you serve as a better role model by keeping out of your husband's business affairs and concentrating on being a good mother to Chelsea and—as hard as it can be at times—a supportive wife?

JESSE JACKSON

When I debated Jesse Jackson on CNN in January 1994, I was very curious to see him in action. Up until the late 1980s when I started getting politically active, I honestly didn't know much about him. All I knew was that he worked with Martin Luther King, Jr., in the 1960s and was supposed to have all the answers for our social ills. He didn't have any idea who I was, except for the brief description CNN gave— "ex-welfare mom." He must have seen that and figured I was a Jesse Jackson groupie. Boy, did he have another thing coming.

The topic on the table that day was black-on-black crime. Reverend Jackson immediately started talking about "demilitarizing" urban communities, which I interpreted as code for gun control. When the host finally asked what I was thinking, I asked how we could confiscate guns from law-abiding citizens when gangsters have no intention of giving up their weapons?

Reverend Jackson and I didn't agree on one subject. He said blacks were isolated and forgotten by the Reagan and Bush administrations. I argued that a reason for the chaos in black neighborhoods is that many blacks feel disconnected from the black Democratic leadership, which has been running the show for decades.

He blamed the GOP for all the poverty and crime in the inner city. I contended that the crisis had less to do with a reduction in social programs than the glaring absence of morality and spirituality in many urban households.

Reverend Jackson came back with the retort that big business had divested $264 billion from urban communities. I said, why is it so hard for liberals like him to recognize the rise in black entrepreneurship and develop ideas for small businesses to employ more young people?

I started getting very irritated when Reverend Jackson began to patronize me. "Don't be mad, let's be rational," he said to me. I fired back irately, "It's hard to be rational living in the effects of what you have been promoting for the last twenty years. It is very hard to see you come out to Los

Angeles and talk about what the gangsters need and how they have been victimized and neglected."

Like all lewd leftists, Jackson insists that government must provide all the solutions, no matter what the cost. He rattled off a list of the usual spend, spend, spend solutions to reduce inner city crime: an urban policy with youth initiatives, an economic development base that included recreation and arts for the kids and jobs for the parents and business options. This isn't just his answer to reduce crime, this is his answer for everything. More welfare, more programs, which lead to more problems. This is exactly what government has been doing for thirty years with nothing to show for it.

More government spending is not the solution. We have enough government in our inner cities already and it's time to wean off it. I told Reverend Jackson that it's going to take more than a new slate of social programs to stop the crime and the deterioration. What's going on in Los Angeles and other cities across America is an all-encompassing break-down: in family values, morality, education, and the work ethic. I said if we don't provide any vision to our young people, they will perish.

In conclusion, I said criminal behavior is contrary to black culture, contrary to what our ancestors in this country stood for. Yet all we hear from black leaders today is that it's somebody else's fault. It's time to look internally and develop our own solutions.

Whoops, there I go sounding like Louis Farrakhan again. But really folks, how many more trillions do we need to spend on stamping out poverty before we realize that there's a better way to address impoverishment and unemployment?

After the television cameras were off, I had to ask Reverend Jackson why he had campaigned against our California school choice ballot initiative two months earlier. Now I was expect-ing a "rational" explanation from the reverend, but he brushed me off. "Well, we won," he shrugged without saying anything else. I said, "But our community took a loss. You sold out your own people."

As I left the studio, I came to the conclusion that Reverend Jackson has another agenda besides curing the ills affecting our inner cities. He's fallen, he's gone, he doesn't represent us anymore.

REACHING OUT TO BLACKS IN THE TWENTY-FIRST CENTURY

It won't be an easy task for white Republicans to persuade black voters to support GOP candidates. One problem for the GOP is its legacy of insensitivity toward black issues. Edmund Peterson, a black public official who worked for President Bush in the Energy Department, has observed that the Republican Party stood on the sidelines during the 1960s civil rights movement and has been paying for it ever since.

He's absolutely right. In the name of states' rights, the GOP shunned the movement at a time when many blacks could not vote or get access to private and public institutions that discriminated on the basis of color. As blacks were abused, Republicans sat by idly and let radical Democrats take the initiative to correct the wrongs. It was a moral and tactical blunder and blacks have not forgotten.

It's a legacy that came back to haunt the GOP in early 1995 after the Republicans took control of Congress. Their desire to reduce the budget deficit, coupled with their endorsement of policies supporting a strong work ethic and self-reliance, was interpreted by the liberal media and the civil rights establishment as lack of sympathy for the poor. Voters have flinched, the Republicans have run scared, and meaningful deficit reduction has been put on the back burner.

The GOP also made a series of bad choices, such as attempting to dismantle affirmative action right away. When Republicans swept the House in 1994, middle-class blacks were voting Republican in record numbers in many congressional districts. Many Republican gubernatorial candidates, such as Wisconsin's Tommy Thompson, also reaped the benefits of the black conservative vote. But undermining affirmative action programs—such as California governor Pete Wilson's drive to remove color as a factor in admissions to state universities—left the indelible impression that the GOP was taking direct aim at middle-class blacks, the very group they needed to attract.

While race-based laws are wrong, I don't have a problem with employers choosing to expand their work force with minorities to increase diversity. But there should be no laws encouraging or discouraging those types of entrepreneurial choices.

In education, the objective should be to increase minority representation without resorting to dumbing down standards. For instance, colleges shouldn't lower academic standards to meet racial quotas, they should get involved with elementary and secondary schools to identify minority kids with college potential and track them so they meet college requirements by graduation time.

It may mean that universities will have to set up their own prep schools to maintain their numbers. That kind of attention to detail could rectify the real problem: low-quality education in our government secondary schools.

However, I also feel government should be able to run itself like a business, including exercising the right to refuse contracts to businesses that don't hire minorities if that is a requirement for eligibility. Period.

Marketing and the GOP

It's ironic that the GOP, the so-called party for business and wealth, has no discernible strategy to market its product to black voters. Like salesmen walking new turf, they should go out and wine and dine their potential clients.

Let's start with the product: conservatism. The GOP needs to say it has a good product, the best on the market, and here's why and how it operates.

I am astonished when I talk to many Republicans who act like they don't understand black people, as if we're some foreign entity. Yet we want the same things as white voters: nice homes, safe neighborhoods, good schools, economic opportunity, and solid families built on the strong moral foundation we hear about in church every Sunday. The GOP is the one party that can perpetuate this environment because we endorse a conservative philosophy that enhances these values. We also want to reduce taxes, limit business regulation, increase personal responsibility, promote self-reliance, and get tougher on criminals. These ideas need to be promoted and the salesmen should be people who understand black neighborhoods.

Finance Conservative Black Candidates

Speaking of money well spent, we need to identify and fund black conservatives to run against opponents from the two groups that have dominated the African-American agenda for decades: the Congressional Black Caucus and the civil rights establishment. The GOP has a golden opportunity to chip away at the foundation of these groups because black voters are taking a critical look at the welfare state too, and many are coming to the same conclusion as other Americans: that social welfare programs have failed the poor.

Republicans, however, need to take note: Among blacks, the political figure gaining the most momentum is Louis Farrakhan. The irony is that one of the main reasons the Muslim movement is thriving is because of it's adherence to conservative values. That is the common ground that needs to be tilled, and the GOP missed a great opportunity to do so by shunning Alan Keyes.

Republicans could reach out to black voters by extending invitations to the heads of inner-city community-based organizations to speak before Congressional committees. Too often, white and black academicians control the information flow instead of the folks with the self-help solutions that provide hope to urban dwellers.

The GOP needs to go to the churches and schools, hold town hall meetings, and fund local organizations and alternative candidates. Jack Kemp's visit to Harlem last September was a terrific example of this, but it must be done on a wider scale. While conservative principles have much to offer black neighborhoods, you can be damn sure the liberal media won't be delivering the news.

The people are ready for another voice. The question is whether the old-guard GOP is ready to share the round table with people who don't think like they do.

AFTERWORD

A Call to Black Conservatives—Onward!

The Heritage Foundation has calculated that this country has spent trillions in the War on Poverty. Clearly, somebody is getting that money and it's not the poor. All along, poverty has been increasing and quite frankly, I'm sick of wasting my money on failed government programs. Hey, there are a million black folks in America making over $50,000 a year and they ought to be sick of it, too.

There are an overwhelming number of black conservatives in this country, but many are still in the closet because they don't want to show white America that there's a break in the ranks. I've broken the code of silence and some folks are angry with me about that. But how can we continue to promote ourselves as victims of racism when despite our long, hard journey through slavery, Jim Crow, and the civil rights era, we now boast a population that circulates more than $400 billion annually in the United States? I can't cry racism when such success has occurred against all odds.

Capitalism is the answer. It has worked for me and many other entrepreneurs. Contrary to what the lewd left likes to promote, we don't need affirmative action to succeed. What we haven't told our people is that they can start their own businesses instead of always relying on government.

I know millions of blacks believe as I do, so it doesn't bother me when I cross a few who don't. That's the message I want to give every time I appear on a television news show or speak before a group of students at a college forum.

The first time I had my chance to do this before a national cable television audience came on January 5, 1994. As I mentioned in Chapter 11, I was in Washington, D.C., with a group of young black conservatives to announce the release of a policy paper on the state of black America. I wondered whether anyone in Washington would read it, or even care about what a group of young black conservatives had to say about capitalism, crime, taxation, and the budget deficit. At the press conference, I stood in a conference room with men like Horace Cooper, at the time the legislative director for Republican congressman Dick Armey of Texas. He said that when liberal black leaders get together they talk about creating government programs to solve problems, and ignore the power of individual initiative. I knew what he was talking about. For me, it was ambition, not a freebie, that drove me to start my Christian magazine.

There was a young man named Stuart DeVeaux, a twenty-three-year-old senior at Howard University. He believed that young black people aren't looking to latch on to gimmee-it-now programs, but are looking for opportunity.

There was a crowd of us and only one podium, so we had to take turns coming forward to speak. I stepped up to the microphone dressed in a low-key gray conservative suit—a rare departure from my flashy wardrobe—and talked about my area of personal experience, welfare and black entrepreneurship.

I said, "We forget that McDonald's started out as a single hamburger stand and that we need to grasp capitalism, even on a small scale, to develop poor neighborhoods. It is the small-business person who is the number one provider of new jobs, not the big corporations. They're not the primary employers of young black men; that will be up to us. The black middle class is going to get hold of this concept either now or when they're standing in the unemployment line."

As a businesswoman, I've devoted a lot of time to this issue. In the seventies, there was a heavy push to integrate blacks into mainstream corporate America through affirmative action, but because of discrimination, the chief employer opening up white-collar opportunities was the government. At the expense of entrepreneurship, massive numbers of blacks started going to college for training in social work and teaching.

These days, black kids can tell you all about government jobs. They call it "working for the man," and the reluctance to follow their parents' footsteps into the public sector has created not only a generation gap, but also an employment gap. Many black youths are going so far as to shun school because the only reward they perceive is a government job. If that is all that's out there for them, no wonder so many young people are questioning the value of an education and choosing a life on the street, hustling for an easy buck. Sadly, the concept of entrepreneurship and how the free market system works is foreign to many blacks, and perhaps even discounted by a generation of black government employees.

As black conservatives, we have a job before us that's a lot bigger than we may realize. Our cities and schools are in need of drastic overhaul. Racial divisiveness is at an all-time high. Black citizens often don't vote, and many of our young leaders are horrible moral examples.

Our first job is to build a foundation of conservatism with strong leaders who can articulate conservative opinions on a variety of issues. They need to be able to talk about why welfare is wrong and how the cycle of dependency is enslaving blacks. They need to be able to speak on the virtues of entrepreneurship, school choice vouchers, and why affirmative action, over the long haul, is detrimental to the economic future of America.

Black conservatives, all our leaders for that matter, must place a higher priority on maintaining a morally impeccable character. We don't need another Mel Reynolds type—highly educated yet hitting on teenage girls, and then mitigating his actions by claiming he's a victim of racism and overzealous police and prosecutors. We need black models of family life where the husband provides leadership and authority, the wife helps nurture and encourage, and the children learn. Those are our chief responsibilities, and we can't allow immoral influences to corrupt our mission.

I don't mean to sermonize, but if you're a father, you provide for your family, and that's it. If you're married, you're faithful. If you're a parent, you set an example. If you're successful in business, you're generous and give something back to the community from which you profit. If you're an employee, you're diligent. If you're a public figure, you're a servant. You give to charity and get your opinion pieces published in newspapers.

This country is morally bankrupt and desperate for new leaders. We're at a crossroads now, with one path heading for moral law and the other to martial law. A military state. Is that what we want? That's what we got in Los Angeles; when the looters and the burners got control, the National Guard was brought in. Are we ready for that? As we face the new millenium, I suggest we define a common culture rooted in moral law, and go from there to rebuild our society.

Americans want to work out their differences and black conservatives are the epitome of the solution. We have felt the sting of urban socialism and know the antidote is capitalism, coupled with a dedication to moral absolutes. It's that combination that stirs hope in all of us and provides the strength to root out racial hatred and replant it with faith in the American Dream.

AFTERWORD ACKNOWLEDGMENTS

Long before I ever contemplated doing a book, there was a group of individuals who helped me turn around my life. Without them, getting off welfare and starting my own business would have been much harder. I mentioned many of you in this memoir and I thank you for eternity.

I also want to extend a heartfelt regards to those who contributed in their own special way:

Frankie Morrow of Independent Management Assistance and her thorough team of transcribers: Doddy Ellis, Kurt Fries and John Kalenda; Bishop Randy Adler; Diana Banister; David Barton; Gary Bauer; Aimee and Hannah Benet; Gail Blocker; Rosa Bravo; Horace Cooper; James Dobson; Joe Farrah; John Fund; George Grant; Avis, Doris, Eric, James, Michael, Vera and Warreno Irby; Stella Greene; James Kennedy; Bishop Douglas Kessler; Amy Mortiz; Phyllis Berry Myers; Mendez Napoli; Ron Nehring; Bob Noonan; Norm Olsen; Jay Parker; Roxanne Petteway; Mark Rubin; Fred and Ruth Sacher; Beverly, Lou and Steve Sheldon; Lyndon Stambler; Cal Thomas; Jerri White; Alvin Williams; Ken Wilson; and Elizabeth Wright.